ID0983459

# THE ID AND THE REGULATORY
# PRINCIPLES OF MENTAL FUNCTIONING

*Journal of the American Psychoanalytic Association*
*Monograph Series Number Four*

# THE ID AND THE REGULATORY PRINCIPLES OF MENTAL FUNCTIONING

## *MAX SCHUR, M.D.*

*International Universities Press, Inc.*

NEW YORK                    NEW YORK

# Contents

# CONTENTS

[ 6 ]

# Foreword

THIS MONOGRAPH, the fourth in the Journal of the American Psychoanalytic Association series, reflects the *Zeitgeist*. During this period of reappraisal of basic psychoanalytic concepts in the light of recent advances in our discipline, it was inevitable that efforts would be directed toward a re-examination of the concept of the id. This historically important concept actually remains less clear and specific in its definition than the other psychic structures. Max Schur's earlier contributions had confronted him with the need to formulate a more integrated concept of id operations. He does so now by boldly taking a stand in favor of a structured id, thus taking a position which is bound to arouse controversy.

The first part of the monograph consists of an exhaustive review which serves to clarify the least well-defined aspect of this psychic system, including the contradictions it embodies. Moreover, in the process of tracing the historical development of this concept, Schur integrates the original concept of the id with the unconscious and the primary process through which it operates and with later contributions to the theory of instinctual drives. He re-evaluates and broadens the concept of the id, viewing it as a constantly developing structure which has adaptive and survival functions. He takes the stand that certain autonomous apparatuses serve the development of the id as well as that of the ego. He re-

[7]

emphasizes Freud's view that there are no strict boundaries between id and ego, or between physiological needs and their mental representations, the latter conceptualized as drives and wishes.

The second part of the monograph is devoted to the regulatory principles of the mind. Here Dr. Schur distinguishes between the pleasure and unpleasure principles as regulatory principles and the affective experience of pleasure and unpleasure. In doing so, he views the unpleasure principle as operating to eliminate disturbances of equilibrium arising mainly from excessive external stimulation. The pleasure principle regulates the need "to recreate, by action or fantasy, any situation which has created the experience of satisfaction." Finally, he re-examines the repetition compulsion and takes the stand that the tendency toward repetition exists in many forms. One of its manifestations is related to the primitive ego defense mechanism of undoing. He suggests the term "compulsive repetitiveness," to replace "repetition compulsion."

It is clear that Dr. Schur not only re-evaluates the concept of the id, but enriches it, in this scholarly, imaginative, and thought-provoking work. He endows it with dimensions derived from a lifelong experience with psyche and soma. It is out of such an approach to psychoanalytic concepts that there arises the concept of a continuum as essential to the understanding of all psychic phenomena. This monograph was conceived by an analyst whose thinking, although adhering to the framework of Freud's fundamental contributions, takes bold steps forward in the elaboration of these contributions.

THE EDITORS

# Author's Note

I WISH TO express my warmest gratitude to Dr. John Frosch and the entire Editorial Board for their encouragement to write this book and for their valuable suggestions. I am especially grateful to Drs. Charles Fisher, Merton Gill, and Edith Jacobson for their patience in reading various versions of the manuscript and for the constructive criticism they provided.

Mrs. Lottie Newman's contribution to this book exceeds by far what is usually called "editorial assistance."

I also thank Mrs. Lucille Osterweil for her patience and tireless work in preparing and editing the successive manuscripts.

This monograph has been supported in part by a grant from the Foundation for Research in Psychoanalysis, Beverly Hills, California.

# Introduction

PSYCHOANALYTIC theory, like that of any branch of science, is in constant need of re-examination. Hartmann, Kris, and Loewenstein have stated this need as follows:

> Concern with clarification of terms is unpopular among psychoanalysts and rare in psychoanalytic writing. This is partly due to Freud's example. Semantics could hardly be the concern of the great explorer, and some inconsistency in the usage of words may well be considered the prerogative of genius. It is a different matter when a generation or two of scientists assume a similar prerogative. . . . Since scientific communication is impaired by ambiguity of meaning, the need for clarification has become urgent [1946, pp. 27, 28].

The clarification of theoretical concepts is never—or at least *should* never be—a pure exercise in semantics. It should on the one hand strive to arrive at formulations which make for progress in theory, and on the other contribute directly or indirectly to a better application of theory—in our science, the teaching and practice of psychoanalysis.

An added goal of clarifying our theoretical concepts may also be to bridge conceptual gaps and eliminate misunderstandings between psychoanalysis and other branches of psychology and the behavioral sciences.

Whenever we attempt to reconsider some of our more basic theoretical concepts, we run up against several obstacles.

[ 11 ]

First of all, we must trace their development in Freud's work where we encounter formulations which occasionally seem contradictory, but which more frequently represent repeated revisions by Freud of previously formulated concepts. Another difficulty arises from the fact that Freud used several frames of reference in attempting to formulate his theories about the working of the mental apparatus.

Freud was of course attempting to find a conceptual framework within which most psychoanalytic formulations could be expressed when he outlined his three metapsychological points of view in "The Unconscious" (1915c), saying: "We see how we have gradually been led into adopting a third point of view in our account of psychical phenomena. Besides the dynamic and the topographical points of view, we have adopted the *economic* one" (p. 181).

When Freud arrived at his structural formulations, the topographical point of view was to some extent replaced by the structural one. From his earliest work Freud was preoccupied with genetic (phylogenetic and ontogenetic), developmental formulations, indispensable for an understanding of most psychoanalytic concepts. It was therefore only natural to add the genetic point of view to the essential metapsychological concepts.

While Freud never neglected problems of adaptation, Hartmann (1939, 1956b, 1964) systematically applied psychoanalytic concepts to adaptation. Realizing the significance of Hartmann's work, Rapaport and Gill (1959) suggested that the adaptive point of view be added to the basic and essential psychoanalytic formulations.

The application of the five metapsychological points of view (genetic, economic, dynamic, structural, adaptive) permits us to place *most*[1] theoretical and clinical concepts within

[1] It is, for example, not easy to apply all the metapsychological points of view to the "regulatory principles" of mental functioning.

[ 12 ]

a proper framework. This applies to such diverse concepts as repression, regression, conflict, symptom formation, sublimation, neutralization, desomatization and resomatization, and so forth.

While the various metapsychological points of view have been applied in considering *all* such concepts, each of the individual points of view has also been the subject of discussion and research. Two in particular have been in the forefront of our interest.

The genetic point of view has been—and still is—the stimulus for all the developmental research carried out in ever-widening areas by both analysts and nonanalysts.

The structural point of view has been the center of our interest to such an extent that we often encounter the term "structural theory" as a substitute for "the structural point of view of metapsychology" (see, for example, Arlow and Brenner, 1964). This interest, as we shall see shortly, originated in an increasing recognition of the importance of the ego in mental functioning. This development could not have taken place without a parallel diminution of interest in the structure id. A *critical evaluation* of the concept "id" in psychoanalytic theory—undertaken more than forty years after Freud formulated his structural concept in *The Ego and the Id* (1923)—is *one* of the main tasks of this study.

The discussion of the concept id which follows will place special emphasis on genetic considerations, while attempting not to neglect the other metapsychological points of view. Apart from these various strictly metapsychological formulations, Freud and all other analysts have used the concepts of certain "regulatory principles" which determine mental functioning.

The concepts "pleasure and unpleasure principles"[2] are of

2 The use of the plural "principles" implies that I am making a certain distinction between these two, as I shall discuss at some length in Chapter 11.

[ 13 ]

course integral to any discussion of the concept id. However, any examination of the regulatory principles would be incomplete without a critical reconsideration of the other regulatory principles set forth by Freud, such as the "Nirvana principle" and, more particularly, the "repetition compulsion." These latter "principles" are in turn inseparable from Freud's theories about the instinctual drives, which are highly pertinent to any discussion of the concept id.

With regard to the reality principle, however, I shall add little to what has already been so exhaustively covered by Hartmann (1956a).

*Part I*

After Freud had formulated the structural point of view, his evaluation of the ego's "strength" in relation to the id underwent a gradual shift.

In one of his first formulations pertaining to this problem, Freud used the famous metaphor of a rider and his horse to describe the mutual relationship between the ego and the id.

> The functional importance of the ego is manifested in the fact that normally control over the approaches to motility devolves upon it. Thus in its relation to the id it is like a man on horseback, who has to hold in check the superior strength of the horse; with this difference, that the rider tries to do so with his own strength while the ego uses borrowed forces. The analogy may be carried a little further. Often a rider, if he is not to be parted from his horse, is obliged to guide it where it wants to go; so in the same way the ego is in the habit of transforming the id's will into action as if it were its own [1923, p. 25].

However, in the same essay Freud also described the relative strength of the ego somewhat differently: "The ego develops from perceiving instincts to controlling them, from obeying instincts to inhibiting them" (pp. 55-56). His view of the impact of analytic therapy on this relation between ego and id was that: "Psycho-analysis is an instrument to enable the ego to achieve a progressive conquest of the id" (p. 56).

Freud reaffirmed and further explained the ego's power in *Inhibitions, Symptoms and Anxiety* (1926), where he illustrated the ego's "very extensive influence over processes in the id" by means of the following metaphor:

> We are very apt to think of the ego as powerless against the id; but when it is opposed to an instinctual process in the id it has only to give a *'signal of unpleasure'* in order to attain its object with the aid of that almost omnipotent institution, the pleasure principle [p. 92].

[ 19 ]

[He concluded:] At this point it is relevant to ask how I can reconcile this acknowledgement of the might of the ego with the description of its position which I gave in *The Ego and the Id*. In that book I drew a picture of its dependent relationship to the id and to the super-ego and revealed how powerless and apprehensive it was in regard to both and with what an effort it maintained its show of superiority over them. This view has been widely echoed in psycho-analytic literature. Many writers have laid much stress on the weakness of the ego in relation to the id and of our rational elements in the face of the daemonic forces within us; and they display a strong tendency to make what I have said into a corner-stone of a psycho-analytic *Weltanschauung*. Yet surely the psycho-analyst, with his knowledge of the way in which repression works, should, of all people, be restrained from adopting such an extreme and one-sided view [p. 95].

*The Future of an Illusion* continued this trend in Freud's thinking. Although Freud was seemingly merciless with all the illusions of humanity, the work ends on a triumphant note of conviction that the primacy of the intellect, the ego, will ultimately prevail.

We may insist as often as we like that man's intellect is powerless in comparison with his instinctual life, and we may be right in this. Nevertheless, there is something peculiar about this weakness. The voice of the intellect is a soft one, but it does not rest till it has gained a hearing. Finally, after a countless succession of rebuffs, it succeeds. This is one of the few points on which one may be optimistic about the future of mankind, but it is in itself a point of no small importance. And from it one can derive yet other hopes. The primacy of the intellect lies, it is true, in a distant, distant future, but probably not in an *infinitely* distant one. . . . Our God, Λόγος [Logos], will fulfil whichever of these wishes nature outside us allows, but he will do it very gradually, only in the unforeseeable future, and for a new generation of men [1927, pp. 53-54].

[ 20 ]

The following letter, written by Freud in 1928, indicates that the "reaffirmation" of the importance of the ego—to use his own words—had progressed to an increasing partiality for the "primacy of the intellect," the ego.

Vienna IX, Berggasse 19
October 4, 1928

My dear Doctor:
I have become aware of the fact that I have neglected to express my thanks for your latest book;[2] I hope, however, that it is not too late to make up for this omission. It was due not to any lack of interest in either its contents or its author, whom I have now learned to appreciate as a humanitarian as well. It arose rather as the result of an uncompleted train of thought which preoccupied me for quite some time after reading the book, and which was predominantly subjective in nature. Despite my unreserved admiration for your warm feelings, your empathy, and your goals, I nevertheless found myself in a kind of opposition which was not easy for me to understand. Ultimately I had to confess to myself that it is caused by the fact that I do not care for these patients [psychotics], that they annoy me, and that I find them alien to me and to everything human. A peculiar kind of intolerance which undoubtedly disqualifies me as a psychiatrist.

In the course of time I have stopped finding myself interesting—something which is certainly analytically incorrect—and have therefore not gotten very far with an explanation of this attitude. Can you understand me better? Am I behaving in this instance as the physicians of yesterday did toward hysterics? *Is this the consequence of an increasingly evident partiality for the primacy of the in-*

2 The letter was addressed to I. Hollos, whose book, *Hinter der gelben Mauer* (Stuttgart: Hyppokrates Verlag, 1928), dealt with the problems of psychosis and mental institutions. I am indebted to the Sigmund Freud Copyright Ltd. for permission to publish this letter.

*tellect, the expression of an animosity toward the id?*[3] Or
what else?

With belated heartiest thanks and many regards,

Your

Freud

Lieber Herr Doktor,

Aufmerksam gemacht, dass ich es unterlassen habe, mich
für Ihr letztes Buch zu bedanken, will ich hoffen, dass es
nicht zu spät ist, das Versäumnis gutzumachen. Es ent-
stammte nicht dem Mangel an Interesse für den Inhalt
oder für den Autor, den ich hier auch als Menschenfreund
schätzen lernte, sondern ergab sich als Folge unabgeschlos-
sener Gedankengänge, die mich nach der Lektüre lange
beschäftigten, die wesentlich subjektiver Natur waren. Bei
uneingeschränkter Anerkennung Ihrer Gefühlswärme,
Ihres Verständnisses und Ihrer Tendenz fand ich mich
doch in einer Art von Opposition, die mir nicht leicht
verständlich wurde. Ich gestand mir endlich, es komme
daher, dass ich diese Kranken nicht liebe, dass ich mich
über sie ärgere, sie so fern von mir und allem Menschlichen
empfinde. Eine merkwürdige Art von Intoleranz, die mich
gewiss zum Psychiater untauglich macht.

Im Laufe der Zeit habe ich aufgehört, mich selbst in-
teressant zu finden, was gewiss analytisch inkorrekt ist, und
bin darum in der Erklärung dieser Einstellung nicht
weiter gekommen. Können Sie mich besser verstehen?
Benehme ich mich dabei wie frühere Ärzte gegen die Hys-
teriker, ist es die Folge einer immer deutlicher gewordenen
Parteinahme für den Primat des Intellekts, den Ausdruck
einer Feindseligkeit gegen das Es? Oder was sonst?

Mit nachträglichem herzlichem Dank u vielen Grüssen

Ihr

Freud

The same trend indicated in this letter is shown in Freud's
famous statement: "Where id was, there ego shall be" (1933,
p. 80).

Freud's aphoristic statement may be paraphrased: the id
has so far not been "replaced" by the ego in evolution. The

3 Italics added.

notion that it can or even should be so replaced is based on a misinterpretation of Freud's aphorism. He could only have meant that the ego may, through analysis, gain access to its unconscious defenses, and also to some of the "dynamic unconscious" (Strachey, 1961; Gill, 1963). The result is an increase in ego autonomy.

What has happened, however, is that in our theoretical formulations much territory formerly ascribed to the id has now been ceded to the ego.

Our generation has been preoccupied with the role of the ego in mental functioning, and rightly so. This preoccupation has resulted in most significant advances in the theory and practice of psychoanalysis. As a result of this preoccupation, however, the concept ego has—to use a metaphor[4]— kept crowding out the other two structures, especially the id. That this preoccupation originated to a certain extent with Freud himself is demonstrated by the previously quoted passages and his letter to Hollos.

Only in Freud's last work was this trend reversed (see Chapter 4). In the *Outline* Freud once again called the id the most important part of the mental apparatus.

When Hartmann, Kris, and Loewenstein attempted their re-examination and clarification of Freud's concepts on the formation of psychic structure, they stated: "We are . . . concerned less with problems of libidinal development, its stages and its manifestations, and more with some problems of ego development and superego formation" (1946, p. 29).

That the concept id is in need of such clarification has also been acknowledged by the fact that the American Psychoanalytic Association devoted a panel discussion to the subject at its annual meeting in Toronto in 1962 (see Marcovitz, 1963).

---

[4] I refer here to the difference between the occasionally unavoidable and therefore legitimate use of metaphors and their frequent objectionable use, as discussed by Hartmann, Kris, and Loewenstein (1946, pp. 32-33).

# 2

## The History of the Concept Id

THE HISTORY of the concept id, which is, at least in part, intimately connected with the history of other structural concepts, has been discussed extensively by Strachey (1961), Hartmann, Kris, and Loewenstein (1946), Beres (1962), and quite recently by Gill (1963). Therefore, I shall deal with it only briefly.

Until the early '20s, Freud's scientific interest, diverse as it was, centered on the uncovering of "the unconscious." Throughout his life he considered his most crucial discovery to have been the realization that most of what is "mental" is unconscious. Freud's conceptualization of the unconscious, which he always considered the cornerstone of psychoanalytic theory, resulted from observations of varied manifestations of normal and abnormal functioning, such as parapraxes, dreams, and neurotic symptoms. He arrived gradually at a distinction between the preconscious and the hardly accessible core of the unconscious—the "dynamic unconscious" (see Strachey, 1961; Gill, 1963)—which can become conscious only after the overcoming of resistances.

The discovery of the "unconscious" was only the first step, however. Freud had to find avenues to an understanding of the unconscious. He had to discern that there was "method in its madness," to find the way it operated. Freud described this mode of operation as the "primary process." He had to assume that this operation had *energies* at its disposal for its

[ 24 ]

functioning, that these energies had their *source* and their *force*. By exerting *pressure* on the executive apparatus, this force becomes a factor motivating behavior. These assumptions were then conceptualized as the "instinctual drives."[1] Freud himself not only described the successive steps by which he formulated his crucially important ideas, but he also told us of some critical stages in their development (1914, 1925b). However, we owe it to Marie Bonaparte that we and future generations have been given the opportunity to relive that development. What I have in mind, of course, is her rescuing Freud's letters to Fliess from destruction (see Schur, 1965a). Through these letters we can participate in the unfolding of Freud's discoveries, in his first completed interpretation of a dream, in his disappointments, in his recognition that he had to overcome not only his patients' but his own resistances, in his embarking on what was perhaps his most heroic and unique feat—his self analysis. His own analysis helped him become aware of the fact that his patients were frequently lying to him in talking about early sexual seduction; it helped him to turn what might have been a crushing defeat into continued progress through such new discoveries as "psychic reality," the intrinsic character of infantile fantasy, infantile sexuality. It led to the realiza-

---

[1] Throughout this paper, Freud's term *"Trieb"* will be translated as "instinctual drive." The use of the term "instinct," which unfortunately—albeit "reluctantly"—is used throughout the *Standard Edition*, has been a source of endless confusion. (See Hartmann, 1939; Hartmann, Kris, and Loewenstein, 1946; Rapaport, 1960a; Waelder, 1960; Schur, 1960a, 1961a; Gill, 1963. This has also been recognized by a research team of the Hampstead Clinic, under Dr. Humberto Nagera.) "Instinct," a term which is frowned on by many biologists and biopsychologists because of its emphasis on the "innate" and its disregard for the "acquired" (Schneirla, 1956), can best be defined as species-specific behavior patterns based prevalently on innate givens.

The term *Trieb*—instinctual drive—connotes not behavior patterns but the inner forces which motivate them. Whenever the word instinct is included in a quotation, it will be followed by the term "instinctual drives" in brackets.

tion of the existence of multiple determinism and to the concept of complementary series (1905c), which implies that development is a function of the interaction of the "innate" and the "acquired" (of "Fate and Accident"[2] [1912]). These discoveries not only made it possible for Freud to establish the role of infantile sexuality in the etiology of neurosis; they also formed the basis for his theories concerning the development of the mental apparatus and early psychic functioning.

Freud came to see the ontogenetic and phylogenetic aspects of this development, which Hartmann (1939) has so aptly called the formation of the inner world through the process of internalization. These formulations laid the groundwork for the "genetic point of view" of metapsychology (Rapaport and Gill, 1959). With them, psychoanalysis has developed from a method of treating neurosis to one of the main representatives of "developmental psychology" (see Hartmann, 1939; Rapaport, 1960b; Schur, 1960b).

In my subsequent discussion (see especially Chapter 7), I shall point to the ways in which close attention to the development of the genetic aspects of Freud's theories may help us clarify our understanding of the concept id.

Freud's clinical observations of repression, resistance, defense, object relations, reality testing, guilt feelings, and so forth, led him to realize that the structural concept had to be added to his metapsychological formulations (1912, 1915a, 1915b, 1915c, 1916-1917, 1917b).

The main reason for abandoning the older topographic or systemic concept was the following: the term "unconscious" had appeared at various times bearing three different meanings. Freud spoke of the "descriptive," the "systemic,"[3] and

[2] Strachey translates these as "Endowment and Chance" (see Freud, 1912, p. 99).

[3] A translation which might be preferable to the generally used and misleading "systematic."

the "dynamic" unconscious, but frequently just of the "system *Ucs.*"[4]

The realization that important manifestations, which had to be attributed to the ego and superego, were also unconscious made a reformulation of that term unavoidable. Freud now (and here I extend a metaphor he used in the *New Introductory Lectures*) had to reapportion the "provinces of the mental apparatus."

Under the new and powerful impression of there being an extensive and important field of mental life which is normally withdrawn from the ego's knowledge so that the processes occurring in it have to be regarded as unconscious in the truly dynamic sense, we have come to understand the term 'unconscious' in a topographical or systematic [systemic] sense as well; we have come to speak of a 'system' of the preconscious and a 'system' of the unconscious, of a conflict between the ego and the system *Ucs.*, and have used the word more and more to denote a mental province rather than a quality of what is mental. The discovery, actually an inconvenient one, that portions of the ego and super-ego as well are unconscious in the dynamic sense, operates at this point as a relief—it makes possible the removal of a complication. We perceive that we have no right to name the mental region that is foreign to the ego 'the system *Ucs.*', since the characteristic of being unconscious is not restricted to it. Very well; we will no longer use the term 'unconscious' in the systematic [systemic] sense and we will give what we have hitherto so described a better name and one no longer open to misunderstanding. Following a verbal usage of Nietzsche's and taking up a suggestion by Georg Groddeck [1923], we will in future call it the 'id'. This impersonal pronoun seems particularly well suited for expressing the main characteristic of this province of the mind—the fact of its being alien to the ego.

4 For a discussion of this, see the Editor's Introduction to and Appendix A of *The Ego and the Id* (1923) in the *Standard Edition*, Vol. XIX, 1961; and especially Gill's excellent and extensive discussion (1963).

The super-ego, the ego and the id—these, then, are the three realms, regions, provinces, into which we divide an individual's mental apparatus, and with the mutual relations of which we shall be concerned in what follows [1933, pp. 71-72].

The ego and the superego were the new structures; their role in mental life preoccupied Freud's thinking. His main "cathexis" was directed toward the "mapping out" of these new provinces. The "reapportionment," as far as the id was concerned, seemed simple. To use the same metaphor, some of the "regions" of the unconscious were assigned to the structures ego and superego. Its main part remained with the id.

# 3

## Ambiguities of the Concept Id

FREUD'S ATTEMPTS at a *general* conceptualization of the id remained somewhat vague. All of them pose many questions and leave the door open to much speculation. We have had to ask ourselves not only: "What did Freud mean by this concept?" but even more important: "How can we fit these conceptualizations into the whole framework of our psychoanalytic theory and practice?"

Apart from various attempts at a general conceptualization, Freud also used the concept id to draw implications and make assumptions that took the more general conceptualization for granted. This also applies to all psychoanalysts who use structural concepts.

Freud's important attempts at conceptualization were the following:

In *The Ego and the Id* (1923) he said:

> I propose to take it into account by calling the entity which starts out from the system *Pcpt.* and begins by being *Pcs.* the 'ego', and by following Groddeck in calling the other part of the mind, into which this entity extends and which behaves as though it were *Ucs.,* the 'id' [p. 23].

The id was said to contain "the passions" (p. 25) and to be "totally non-moral" (p. 54).

In the *New Introductory Lectures* (1933), Freud stated:

> It [the id] is the dark, inaccessible part of our personality; what little we know of it we have learnt from our study of

[ 29 ]

the dream-work and of the construction of neurotic symptoms, and most of that is of a negative character and can be described only as a contrast to the ego. We approach the id with analogies: we call it a chaos, a cauldron full of seething excitations. We picture it as being open at its end to somatic influences,[1] and as there taking up into itself[2] instinctual needs which find their psychical expression in it, but we cannot say in what substratum. It is filled with energy reaching it from the instincts [instinctual drives], but it has no organization, produces no collective will,[3] but only a striving to bring about the satisfaction of the instinctual needs subject to the observance of the pleasure principle. The logical laws of thought do not apply in the id, and this is true above all of the law of contradiction. Contrary impulses exist side by side, without cancelling each other out or diminishing each other: at the most they may converge to form compromises under the dominating economic pressure towards the discharge of energy. There is nothing in the id that could be compared with negation; and we perceive with surprise an exception to the philosophical theorem that space and time are necessary forms of our mental acts. There is nothing in the id that corresponds to the idea of time; there is no recognition of the passage of time, and—a thing that is most remarkable . . . —no alteration in its mental processes is produced by the passage of time. Wishful impulses which have never passed beyond the id, but impressions, too, which have been sunk into the id by repression, are virtually immortal; after the passage of decades they behave as though they had just occurred. They can only be recognized as belonging to the past, can only lose their importance and be deprived of their cathexis of energy, when they have been made conscious by the work of analysis, and it is on this that the therapeutic effect of analytic treatment rests to no small extent [pp. 73-74].

[1] "The somatic sphere" would seem to be a preferable translation of *"das Somatische."*
[2] "And as absorbing there" would seem preferable.
[3] "Uniform" rather than "collective" seems more accurate.

In the *Outline* (1940) Freud said:

We have arrived at our knowledge of this psychical apparatus by studying the individual development of human beings. To the oldest of these psychical provinces or agencies we give the name of *id*. It contains everything that is inherited, that is present at birth, that is laid down in the constitution—above all, therefore, the instincts [instinctual drives], which originate from the somatic organization and which find a first psychical expression here [in the id] in forms unknown to us. [In a footnote Freud added:] This oldest portion of the psychical apparatus remains the most important throughout life; moreover, the investigations of psycho-analysis started with it [p. 145].

We can see that the first attempt at conceptualization in *The Ego and the Id* was the vaguest and most general one. The paragraphs quoted from the *New Introductory Lectures* are much more meaningful. In the *Outline* the concept id is treated more extensively. The paragraphs quoted above contain the more general conceptualizations. However, throughout the *Outline* are scattered many formulations which are directly relevant to an understanding of the concept id.

Let us now enumerate some of the many assumptions common to most attempts at conceptualizing the id.

1. *Most of the attributes of the "system Ucs." are applied to the concept id.*
   *a.* The processes in the id "obey the laws of the primary process."

We can say, therefore, that most of what Freud had to say about this crucially important concept of the primary process, beginning with Chapter VII of *The Interpretation of Dreams,* also applies to his conceptualization of the id. He elaborated on this in the *New Introductory Lectures* (see above), and repeatedly in the *Outline:*

We have found that processes in the unconscious or in the id obey different laws from those in the preconscious ego. We name these laws in their totality the *primary process,* in contrast to the *secondary process* which governs the course of events in the preconscious, in the ego [1940, p. 164].

One further formulation is pertinent to my later discussion:

The core of our being, then, is formed by the obscure *id.* . . . Within this id the organic *instincts* [instinctual drives] operate. . . . The processes which are possible in and between the assumed psychical elements in the id (the *primary process*) differ widely from those which are familiar to us through conscious perception in our intellectual and emotional life; nor are they subject to the critical restrictions of logic, which repudiates some of these processes as invalid and seeks to undo them.

The id, cut off from the external world, has a world of perception of its own. It detects with extraordinary acuteness certain changes in its interior, especially oscillations in the tension of its instinctual needs, and these changes become conscious as feelings in the pleasure-unpleasure series. It is hard to say, to be sure, by what means and with the help of what sensory terminal organs these perceptions come about. But it is an established fact that self-perceptions— coenaesthetic feelings and feelings of pleasure-unpleasure —govern the passage of events in the id with despotic force [1940, pp. 197-198].

  *b.* . In mental life, there is some kind of energy at work.

The energy which operates in the id is a "freely mobile energy" which drives for immediate discharge (1940, p. 164).[4]

From the evidence of the existence of these two tendencies to condensation and displacement our theory infers that in the unconscious id the energy is in a freely mobile state and

---

[4] Gill (1963) suggests the distinction between "free" energy and "mobile" energy. According to him, only the term "free" energy should be used for instinctual energy, while "mobile" energy should be restricted to attention cathexis (hypercathexis). See also Freud (1900, p. 615) who uses the term *"mobile Besetzungsenergie"* in his discussion of attention.

that the id sets more store by the possibility of discharging quantities of excitation than by any other consideration; and our theory makes use of these two peculiarities in defining the character of the primary process we have attributed to the id [1940, p. 168].

 *c.* The id "obeys" the pleasure-unpleasure principle without any restrictions.

2. *The id contains the instinctual drives.*

The most pertinent description of the relationship between the id and the instinctual drives was given in the *New Introductory Lectures* (1933, pp. 73-74; see the quotations above). Similar formulations were made by Anna Freud (1936):

> Unfortunately the passing of instinctual impulses from one institution to the other may be the signal for all manner of conflicts, with the inevitable result that observation of the id is interrupted. On their way to gratification the id-impulses must pass through the territory of the ego and here they are in an alien atmosphere. In the id the so-called 'primary process' prevails; there is no synthesis of ideas, affects are liable to displacement, opposites are not mutually exclusive and may even coincide and condensation occurs as a matter of course. The sovereign principle which governs the psychic processes is that of obtaining pleasure [p. 7].

Hartmann, Kris, and Loewenstein (1946) also emphasized that "Functions of the id are characterized by the great mobility of cathexes of the instinctual *tendencies* and their *mental representatives* [my italics], i.e., by the operation of the primary process. Its manifestations are condensation, displacement, and the use of special symbols" (p. 31). Thus, these authors, too, place "the instinctual drives and their vicissitudes" at the core of their formulations.

Apart from attempts at general conceptualizations, Freud —and subsequently all analysts who have applied the structural concepts—used the concept id not only in manifold formulations of psychoanalytic theory, but in every clinical presentation whenever such terms as conflict, instinctual demands, instinctual danger, and so forth, were involved.

Let us turn first to a discussion of the concept of instinctual drives, which is essential to our understanding of the concept id.[5]

The concepts instinctual drives and id are both rooted in Freud's study of dreams and neurotic symptoms. It will therefore not surprise us to find a great deal about both concepts preformulated in *The Interpretation of Dreams,* especially in Chapter VII.

The uncovering of the dream work, of the fulfillment of infantile, unconscious wishes, and the description of the qualities of the primary process led in two directions, namely, to the first formulation of the "system" *Ucs.* and its qualities (1900), and to the concept of instinctual drives (1905c). After the formulation of the structural concept, the concept id became a kind of synthesis of the two. On the one hand, most of the "qualities" ascribed to the system *Ucs.* were now attributed to the id; on the other hand, the id was said to contain the instinctual drives, which in turn became the "motivational force" inherent in this structure.

Freud introduced the theory of instinctual drive in 1905, in the *Three Essays on the Theory of Sexuality.* However, only in the discussion of the Schreber case (1911a, p. 74), in a passage added to the *Three Essays* in 1914, and finally, in 1915, in "The Instincts and Their Vicissitudes," did he formulate this concept in a psychological framework.

If we now apply ourselves to considering mental life from a *biological* point of view, an 'instinct' [instinctual drive]

[5] For a history and discussion of the instinctual drive concept, see, among others, E. Bibring (1936), Hartmann (1948, 1964), Rapaport (1960b).

appears to us as a concept on the frontier between the mental and the somatic, as the psychical representative of the stimuli originating from within the organism and reaching the mind, as a measure of the demand made upon the mind for work in consequence of its connection with the body [1915a, pp. 121-122].

This formulation, especially the middle part, comprises in an extremely condensed way a series of intermediary steps:

*a.* Stimuli originate "within the organism"; this means, obviously, within the soma.

*b.* These stimuli "reach the mind."

*c.* In the "mind"—we might say in the mental apparatus —these stimuli result in what Freud calls "a psychical representative." (Frequently the term "mental representative" is used, or "psychical expression," as in the earlier quoted passage from the *New Introductory Lectures.*)

The earlier definition, found in the *New Introductory Lectures,* of the concept instinctual drive is now extended to the concept id. We shall see why this definition is so meaningful and why the resolution of any controversy or ambiguity about the concept id hinges on a thorough interpretation of this definition.

This definition does not rule out the fact that some *somatic* processes *must* underlie *all* aspects of mental functioning. Freud discussed this factor extensively in the *Outline,* and I shall come back to it later. However, until we know much more about the correlation of behavior with somatic processes,[6] any constructs derived from our knowledge of the latter must remain vague. We are limited, for the time being, to arriving at concepts about the operation of the mental apparatus mainly through a study of "behavior," in the broadest meaning of

[6] For recent attempts in this direction, see Fisher (1965), Greenfield and Lewis (1965), Hebb (1949), Littman (1958), Marcus (1963), Peters (1958).

[ 35 ]

the term, and will have to confine ourselves to a framework of psychological conceptualization.

Rapaport discussed Freud's definition of an instinctual drive as follows:

> A thoroughgoing psychological determinism—one of the implications of this definition—does not necessitate the assumption of a severance of the mental apparatus from the body, but leads to the following two working assumptions: (a) the laws of functioning of the mental apparatus (i.e., the laws of behavioral regulation) can and must be investigated by a study of behavior (or if you prefer, molar behavior) without reference to molecular, physiological, or neural processes; (b) the relationships of the explanatory constructs derived from behavior to somatic processes must be kept vague at least as long as our knowledge of both types of process is meager, lest psychological concepts (or even behaviors) be prematurely equated with or tied to specific physiological processes [1960a, p. 194].

Freud expressed this view most succinctly when he said:

> By the source [*Quelle*] of an instinct is meant the somatic process which occurs in an organ or part of the body and whose stimulus is represented in mental life by an instinct [instinctual drive]. We do not know whether this process is invariably of a chemical nature or whether it may also correspond to the release of other, e.g. mechanical, forces. . . . An exact knowledge of the sources of an instinct [instinctual drive] *is not invariably necessary for purposes of psychological investigation* . . . [1915a, p. 123; my italics].

I am of course aware how difficult it is to base a special formulation on a specific quotation from Freud, for another quotation may quickly be found to contradict the first one. This applies in particular to both the instinctual drive and id concepts.

Strachey, in an Editor's note to "The Instincts and Their Vicissitudes" (1915a), has pointed to discrepancies between the definition given in that paper and certain formulations found in "Repression" (1915b) and "The Unconscious" (1915c), despite the fact that all of these papers were written within a few weeks of each other.

Freud's formulations in the latter two papers contain contradictions. On the one hand, the instinctual drives were described in energic terms, as a cathexis attached to a "representative" (1915b, p. 148), or to an idea (1915c, p. 177). He even spoke of an idea "which is cathected with a definite quota of psychical energy (libido or interest) coming from an instinct [instinctual drive]" (1915b, p. 152).

On the other hand, we find in "The Unconscious" a separate chapter devoted to "The Special Characteristics of the *Ucs.*" (1915c, pp. 186-189), in which Freud summarized all the qualities ascribed to the *mental processes* localized in "the nucleus of the *Ucs.*" The previously quoted references (at the beginning of this chapter) defining the id are more in line with this definition of instinctual drives which I have taken as a point of departure.

Several explanations can be offered for such shifts in Freud's definitions:

At this time Freud was still expressing his concepts within the framework of the topographic point of view. However, structural formulations were being foreshadowed, especially in his treatment of "repression" proper, "after-pressure" (*Nachdrängen;* 1915b, p. 148) and anticathexis or counter-cathexis.

Freud tried to explain this process in energic terms. All these considerations led him to add the *economic point of view* to his metapsychological presentation. In preparation for the formulation of the economic point of view, the concepts of cathexis, anticathexis, and their vicissitudes gained in emphasis, and with them also the use of the concept psychic energy.

While structural formulations were already discernible in both papers, Freud's theory of affects, specifically of anxiety, was still limited to what Rapaport (1953) has called the second stage of affect theory; e.g., Freud's statement that "affects and emotions correspond to processes of discharge" (1915c, p. 178). He attributed to the system *Pcs.-Cs.* the tendency to control two modes of discharge: motility and affect. He still assumed, too, that both libido and other affects could change to anxiety. The structural theory of anxiety and of the danger concept was not formulated until eleven years later. *He had to rely, therefore, on explanations based mainly on shifts and withdrawals of cathexis.*

Far-reaching conclusions can be drawn from one sentence which designated an instinctual drive as the "psychic representative" of somatic stimuli.

Why should this statement be controversial or sound ambiguous?

The reason may be seen as semantic, but in an especially meaningful sense of the term. A mental representation, according to psychoanalytic theory, is based on a memory trace. A memory trace, in turn, presupposes a perception of a stimulus which may originate from within or without the organism. Perception and memory, however, are generally considered to be ego functions. This seems the crucial ambiguity to be clarified. It is this ambiguity which also characterizes the concept id. Beres, who presented a thoughtful paper at the previously mentioned panel on the concept id (see Marcovitz, 1963), was grappling with the same dilemma. He assumed that Freud "places the instinctual drive in a separate category from its mental expression in the id." Therefore, Beres saw the id as "a step beyond the pure biological drive and not yet [expressing] the *organized* [my italics] wish or fantasy." Beres also re-emphasized Freud's assertion that the energies of the id were "mobile," and that its characteristics were those associated with primary-process discharge (see also Beres, 1965).

To restrict the id—as has been done with the concept "primary process"—to an energy (economic) concept is, of course, a legitimate way out of the dilemma. The consequences of such a view have been discussed by Gill (1963, pp. 132, 144); I shall take them up again later. Beres also stated, however, that we must consider the "problem of mental activity which is 'pre-ego or non-ego.'"

# 4

## General Formulations of the Concept Id

BEFORE elaborating on the crucial ambiguity of the *definitions* of the id, I shall discuss some formulations of the id's over-all importance in mental life, its functions, its energy, and its genesis.

Freud always emphasized that the three "structures" ("provinces") of the mental apparatus were meant to be constructs and were not to be taken literally (1933, p. 79). Although not given to drawing many diagrams,[1] Freud drew two of these to illustrate the "place" of the id in the mental apparatus, one in *The Ego and the Id* (1923), the other in the *New Introductory Lectures* (1933). Significantly, neither diagram showed a strict delineation between the two structures id and ego. This fluid transition conforms to the concept of a continuum which, taken in conjunction with the concept of a complementary series, is so essential for an understanding of all formulations of mental functioning.[2]

While the two diagrams were basically identical, it is inter-

[1] See, for instance, Chapter VII of *The Interpretation of Dreams* (1900, p. 541).

[2] The concept of a continuum permits us to see, for instance, in the whole spectrum of responses from a thoughtlike awareness of potential danger to the panic in a traumatic situation, the hierarchical variations of the anxiety response (Schur, 1953, 1958). The concept of a complementary series permits us to see human development as the result of interaction between innate and experiential factors (Freud, 1905c, 1912; Benjamin, 1961; Anna Freud, 1965).

esting to note that in the later one the ego had "grown" in size compared with the id, and that the area of the "repressed" was more on "common territory," *on the "borderline" between ego and id.* I shall return to this problem (see especially Chapter 8).[3]

The concept of a continuum is also implicit in the following formulation advanced by Hartmann, Kris, and Loewenstein (1946): "Under specific conditions one of the centers [i.e., the three structures] may expand its area, and another or the two others may recede" (p. 30).

The decisive importance of the id was emphasized by Freud again and again, especially in the *Outline*. For example: "This oldest portion of the psychical apparatus remains the most important throughout life" (1940, p. 145, n. 2). Or: "The power of the id expresses the true purpose of the individual organism's life" (1940, p. 148).

This relative importance of the id was expressed partly in topographical or systemic terms (Gill, 1963). The emphasis was on the assumption that only a small part of what is mental is conscious, or even accessible to consciousness. "Psychoanalysis regarded everything mental as being in the first instance unconscious" (1925b, p. 31).

The id's importance is guaranteed by the instinctual drives which fill it with energy. We assume that human behavior is the result of a hierarchical layer of motivational forces (that it is overdetermined). The instinctual drives, however they

3 This growth of the ego area may be in line with Freud's increasing preoccupation with the ego. We might say that Freud applied his famous dictum "Where id was, there ego shall be" (1933, p. 80) to the diagram of his conceptual model. He was cautioning us (and perhaps himself) when he said: "It is certainly hard to say to-day how far the drawing is correct. In one respect it is undoubtedly not. The space occupied by the unconscious id ought to have been incomparably greater than that of the ego or the preconscious. I must ask you to correct it in your thoughts" (1933, p. 79).

may be transformed by ego and superego functions—which in turn also represent environmental influences—are an essential part of this motivation.[4]

The defining characteristics attributed by Freud to the instinctual drives (1915a) are, of course, also essential to the concept id. These characteristics include: (1) pressure; (2) aim; (3) object; and (4) source.

### PRESSURE

By the pressure [*Drang*] of an instinct [instinctual drive] we understand its motor factor, the amount of force or the measure of the demand for work which it represents. The characteristic of exercising pressure is common to all instincts [instinctual drives]; it is in fact their very essence [1915a, p. 122].

Pressure implies force, and force implies energy. A thorough discussion of the concept "psychic energy," as important as this may be, is beyond the scope of this paper. Various aspects have been discussed not only by Freud but by Hartmann (1939, 1950), Hartmann, Kris, and Loewenstein (1949), Fenichel (1945), and many others. Rapaport dealt with this concept in his paper on the psychoanalytic theory of motivation (1960a), comparing (chiefly contrasting) Freud's concept of psychic energy with that of other psychologists who have dealt with this subject. According to Rapaport, the one who came closest to Freud's formulations was Kurt Lewin (1935), when he stated that all concepts of energy, force, tension, and systems employed in psychology were "general logical fundamental concepts of all dynamics . . . in no way a special pos-

---

4 See Bibring (1936); Hartmann (1948); Hartmann, Kris, and Loewenstein (1946, 1949); Loewenstein (1940). For a special discussion of the concept motivation, see Rapaport (1960a).

session of physics" (see Heisenberg, 1958).[5] We must remind ourselves constantly that when we speak about "drives," "energy," etc., we are not speaking of any specific type of physiological energy, but are referring to energy "expended in the initiation, regulation, and termination of behavior" (Rapaport, 1960a).[6]

## AIM AND OBJECT

The aim of an instinctual drive is to obtain "satisfaction" by removing a state of tension (excitation).[7] The object of an instinctual drive is that *"in regard to which or through which the instinct is able to achieve its aim"* (Freud, 1915a, p. 122; my italics). The wording "in regard to which" implies the "direction" of the instinctual drive. An object[8] is "what is most variable about an instinct[ual drive] and is not originally connected with it, but becomes assigned to it only in consequence of being peculiarly fitted to make satisfaction possible" (1915a, p. 122). The variability of objects which are best fitted to enable satisfaction is limited by innate (species-specific) factors. This variability increases in the evolutional series and reaches its peak in man. The inclusion of an object in the characteristics of an instinctual drive necessarily gives a certain teleological aspect to it. What is "teleological," however, is not the explanatory concept but the facts which

5 A certain analogy can be drawn between the use of the concepts energy, function, and structure, and their interrelationships in psychoanalysis and the use of such concepts as energy, function, and matter in atomic physics (see also Schur, 1965b).

6 The same injunction also applies to such concepts as "libidinal," "aggressive" energy, "neutralization" (Hartmann, 1950, 1952), "desomatization" (Schur, 1955), etc.

7 The concept of "satisfaction" is here formulated mainly in economic terms within the framework of the pleasure and unpleasure principles (see Chapters 12, 13, 14).

8 Hoffer (1952) rightly emphasizes the necessity of distinguishing between the *objective* and the *object* of an instinctual drive.

underlie selective evolution and the development of those functional structures which, given an average expectable environment (Hartmann, 1939; Rapaport, 1960a), can best guarantee survival.

SOURCE

Freud relegated the source of the instinctual drives to the domain of physiology. This was inherent in the definition according to which the instinctual drives are the psychical (mental) representatives of stimuli originating within the organism, i.e., the soma.

It is understandably difficult to keep apart the physiological source of the stimuli reaching the mental apparatus and their mental representations, conceptualized as the instinctual drives. The concept of component instinctual drives, which is geared to the description of various aspects of the libidinal "zones" and phases of development, therefore gives the *Three Essays on the Theory of Sexuality* (1905c) a "peripheralistic" aspect.

In Freud's later writings, in which the concepts of Eros and Thanatos[9] emerged (1920, 1923, 1924a), more even than in "Instincts and Their Vicissitudes," this peripheralistic aspect was considerably changed. The physiological sources of libidinal drives were obviously under hormonal influence. The stimulation of various sense organs influenced their "tensions" and "trigger[ed their] discharge." The source and nature of the physiological stimulus would influence their mental representation.[10] For instance, hunger, through its mental representation, might set in motion "oral" libidinal and destructive urges. The musculature was instrumental in

9 When I mention the concept "Thanatos" in this connection, I do not mean to express agreement with Freud's "death instinct" theory.
10 See Chapter 7 for a discussion of the development of a wish.

[ 44 ]

the execution of aggression. However, the libidinal and aggressive instinctual drives were conceived as *mental (psychic) representations* of such "peripheral" sources. These sources eventually came to be conceived of as somatic stimuli in a much more general sense. The rapid development of research in the area of enzyme systems and of various agents which influence synaptic transmission of impulses points to the possibility that the physiology of the "sources" of the instinctual drives will some day be clarified.

Such research as the experimental work done on sleep and dreams (recently surveyed by Fisher, 1965) and on the central localization of certain "instincts" (Lilly, 1960) may also help us establish a bridge between the somatic sources of the instinctual drives, the transmission of somatic impulses to certain apparatuses in the central nervous system, and their function which is in turn the substrate of mental representations of instinctual drives and their derivatives.

I shall return to the problem of "peripheral" versus "central" when I discuss the genetic aspect of the id, specifically the evolutionary aspects of internalization (Chapter 6). The following general considerations may be pertinent at this point, however. The instinctual drives are conceptualized as mental representations of forces originating within the soma. It is inconceivable that the organism should *ab ovo* be equipped with a definite amount of libidinal and aggressive energy in terms of a closed system. The reservoir of instinctual drive energy is replenished *throughout life* in a manner which does not fall within the domain of psychology. It is hard to imagine that the inconsistency of the idea of a "permanent reservoir of libido," which seems to be implied in some of Freud's statements, could have escaped him.

His preoccupation with the death-instinct theory (Nirvana principle) prevented him, perhaps, from arriving at a formulation that would view the organism as an open system.

[ 45 ]

While death as a consequence of a "victory" of "Thanatos" over "Eros" remains speculative, the psychological formulation that death is the consequence of the inability to replenish libidinal and aggressive energies now seems to be in line with the biological concept of death (Schur, 1966).[11]

[11] Shortly before his untimely death, Maxwell Gitelson called my attention to an excerpt in the *Saturday Review* of June 1, 1963 from a collection of essays entitled *Horizons in Biochemistry* published as a tribute to Albert Szent-Gyorgyi. The essay, by D. E. Koshland, Jr., of the Brookhaven National Laboratory, speculates about the possible existence of a "death hormone" as compatible with the theories of enzyme structure and hormone action. "If natural selection is believed, death of the individual provides a mechanism for improvement of the species as a whole. It is nature's way of correcting errors and developing new and more efficient living systems. . . . Where would one look for such a hormone? How would it act? The symptoms of age, e.g., desiccation, decrease in metabolic rates, would seem to provide some clues for experimental approaches to the search for such a hormone. In view of the preceding discussion, the possibility that the 'death hormone' is a general enzyme inhibitor rather than one blocking a specific enzyme, would also seem worthy of consideration. The juvenile hormone apparently acts by inhibiting hormones or enzymes which cause metamorphosis; hence some analogy for such a message of death mechanism can be found."

One wonders what Freud's reaction would have been to such a hypothesis!

# 5

## *The Functions of the Id*

In DESCRIBING the characteristics of the instinctual drives, the "functions" of the id have in part already been indicated. Enumerating the various functions ascribed to the id would mean abstracting not only most of the psychoanalytic literature but *every* psychoanalytic case history. I shall therefore examine only representative formulations.

The most common formulation is that the id "strives" for the satisfaction of what Freud called the individual organism's innate needs (1940, p. 148). The id therefore exerts pressure (see Chapter 4) on the ego to mediate the gratification of these needs. These needs are "rooted in instinctual drives and their vicissitudes" (Hartmann, Kris, and Loewenstein, 1946, p. 31). It follows that they include all the strivings of libido and aggression. Both libido and aggression, in the broadest meaning of these concepts, are integral parts of every aspect of mental functioning. Their manifestations in ideation, affects, thoughts, fantasies, and so forth, depend, on the one hand, on various degrees of instinctual fusion, and, on the other, on the influence of various ego functions (neutralization, reality testing, defenses, etc.).

The id-drives-strivings-demands-derivatives, whatever we may call them (I purposely avoid the term "wishes" before discussing the essential meaning of this crucial concept), need an object for their gratification (discharge). Object relations in all their complexity therefore always have an "id element."

[ 47 ]

While we are speaking of the various assumptions about id functions in general, we must include, especially in the area of object relations, the respective roles of libido and aggression, their vicissitudes, their fusion and defusion.

At this point we may perhaps arrive at the following hypothetical generalization: the concept of a continuum applies to the delineation—or rather to the lack of it—between the structures "ego" and "id." This concept of a continuum, as well as that of complementary series, must also apply to the participation of id elements in all mental functioning. Such participation should be considered not only from a quantitative but also from a qualitative point of view. The validity of these assumptions and their application to certain specific functions, generally described as ego functions, have to be tested in further discussion.

The preceding discussion may also come under the heading of "influence of id on ego development," which is part of the problem of the *mutual* influences in the development of ego and id (the topic of a symposium held at the 17th Congress of the International Psycho-Analytical Association in Amsterdam, 1951; see Anna Freud, 1952; Hartmann, 1952; Hoffer, 1952).

The influence of instinctual development on ego development has been one of the cornerstones of the genetic point of view. While Freud never disregarded the influence of the environment, and spoke about the system *Pcpt.-Cs.* as the "nucleus of the ego" (1923, p. 28, n. 2), the development of thought, action, ideation, the secondary process, censorship, and defense was originally conceived by him as influenced to a great extent either by the need to provide instinctual gratification or by the necessity to inhibit drive discharge.

It is not surprising, therefore, that until 1938 Freud saw the ego as developing "out" of the id. Only in the *Outline* did Freud speak about an "undifferentiated ego-id." The recognition of the mutuality of this development had to wait for the formulation of the concepts of an undifferentiated phase, of primary and secondary autonomy, of neutralization, and of the ego as the organ of adaptation (Hartmann, 1939, 1950, 1952, 1964; Hartmann, Kris, and Loewenstein, 1946).

I likewise assume that there are evolutional and developmental aspects of the id, an assumption I have previously expressed—albeit in passing—in earlier papers and discussions (1958, 1960a, 1963). Every development takes place in interaction with the environment and is also dependent on it. If this is so, the id must have its role in adaptation. It certainly mediates in the adaptive function of the ego through the "pressure" of the instinctual demands (see Hartmann, Kris, and Loewenstein, 1946; Loewenstein, 1940).

I arrive here, in part from different points of departure, at a formulation similar to that of Gill, whose manuscript I read before completing this essay.[1]

The mutual "relationship" between the id and the other structures is also the cornerstone of the concept of conflict, which plays such an important role in psychoanalytic theory of normal and abnormal development.

I must now discuss one more "function" which Freud attributed to the id. He did so in a few, somewhat cryptic paragraphs, which have been rather puzzling to every careful reader, and have frequently invited the criticism of "loose formulation." In *The Ego and the Id* Freud said:

Internal perceptions yield sensations of processes arising in the most diverse and certainly also in the deepest strata

[1] As Gill's monograph (1963) appeared before this one, I shall forego a more detailed discussion of the adaptive aspects of the id and the question of whether even the prototypes of certain defensive structures should be attributed to the id (e.g., thresholds). See also Fisher (1961) and Wolff (1960). Gill has graciously agreed that no "priority claims" should figure in our presentations. I have left many paragraphs of my draft unchanged, at the risk of seeming repetitious.

of the mental apparatus. Very little is known about these sensations and feelings; those belonging to the pleasure-unpleasure series may still be regarded as the best examples of them. They are more primordial, more elementary, than perceptions arising externally, and they can come about even when consciousness is clouded [1923, pp. 21-22].

This statement became more specific in the *Outline,* as can be seen in the paragraph on the id previously quoted (Chapter 3).

These paragraphs bring us right back to the same basic ambiguity which we encountered earlier in the discussion of Freud's definition of instinctual drive (Chapter 3).

It thus has become more and more obvious that the reduction of the id to a pure "energy" concept, if pursued to its logical conclusion, would necessitate a complete reformulation of most psychoanalytic concepts. We might even say that most psychoanalytic papers published since 1923, or even every case history, would have to be rewritten.

Let us see whether a genetic, developmental consideration of the id can bring us any closer to clarification.

# 6

## The Development of the Id

MANY DEVELOPMENTAL formulations about the id are scattered throughout Freud's writings. I shall discuss only the most pertinent ones. In view of the intimate relationship between the concept id and instinctual drives, this part of my discussion applies to the developmental formulations of both.

Freud introduced genetic[1] considerations concerning the mental apparatus in Chapter VII of *The Interpretation of Dreams* (1900). Although these statements are particularly important for my topic, I shall first discuss his later ones. Freud's genetic formulations fall into the following categories:

1. Evolutional
2. Ontogenetic
   a. innate endowment
   b. maturation
   c. development

FREUD'S EVOLUTIONAL FORMULATIONS

In "Instincts and Their Vicissitudes" (1915a) Freud stated:

In order to guide us in dealing with the field of psychological phenomena, we do not merely apply certain conventions to our empirical material as basic *concepts;* we

---

[1] In this monograph I use the term "genetic" to cover both phylogenetic (evolutional) and ontogenetic aspects. The term "developmental" applies only to the development of the phenotype (see Chapter 8).

also make use of a number of complicated *postulates*. We have already alluded to the most important of these, and all we need now do is to state it expressly. This postulate is of a biological nature, and makes use of the concept of 'purpose' (or perhaps of expediency) and runs as follows: the nervous system is an apparatus which has the function of getting rid of the stimuli that reach it, or of reducing them to the lowest possible level; or which, if it were feasible, would maintain itself in an altogether unstimulated condition. Let us . . . assign to the nervous system the task—speaking in general terms—of *mastering stimuli*. We then see how greatly the simple pattern of the physiological reflex is complicated by the introduction of instincts [instinctual drives]. External stimuli impose only the single task of withdrawing[2] from them; this is accomplished by muscular movements, one of which eventually achieves that aim and thereafter . . . becomes a hereditary disposition. Instinctual stimuli, which originate from within the organism, cannot be dealt with by this mechanism. Thus they make far higher demands on the nervous system and cause it to undertake involved and interconnected activities by which the external world is so changed as to afford satisfaction to the internal source of stimulation. Above all, they oblige the nervous system to renounce its ideal intention of keeping off stimuli, for they maintain an incessant and unavoidable afflux of stimulation. We may therefore well conclude that instincts [instinctual drives] and not external stimuli are the true motive forces behind the advances that have led the nervous system, with its unlimited capacities, to its present high level of development. There is naturally nothing to prevent our supposing that the instincts [instinctual drives] themselves are, at least in part, precipitates of the effects of external stimulation, which in the course of phylogenesis have

[2] It is significant that Freud considered "withdrawal" to be the only response to stimuli. In this he follows the *neurological* reflex model and his formulations on the constancy principle. The *physiological* response to stimuli can be "approach" as well as "withdrawal" (Schneirla, 1959; Schur, 1960a, 1960b, 1961a, 1962). For a further discussion, see Chapter 7.

brought about modifications in the living substance [pp. 119-120].

This paragraph is replete with both evolutional implications and outright evolutional assumptions.

The first implication is not immediately obvious. Freud emphasized "how greatly the simple pattern of the physiological reflex is complicated by the introduction of instincts [instinctual drives] . . . which originate from within the organism." In the context of the rest of the quoted paragraph, especially its last sentence, the term "introduction," too, must be understood in evolutional terms.

This formulation is of special importance for our topic *if we apply it to ontogenetic development as well.* In the literature there is a running controversy among representatives of various schools of biology, "biopsychology," and comparative psychology over the relative dependence of behavior on peripheral sensory, as opposed to central, stimulation. As far as human developmental psychology is concerned, Piaget's work, for instance, places great emphasis on sensory input. (See also the experimental work on the influence of sensory deprivation; e.g., Miller, 1962; Klein, 1965.)

There seems to be enough evidence, however, to warrant the following assumption: when we apply the concept of complementary series to the problem "central versus peripheral," we may state that in the evolutional series, with the development of the central nervous system, the *relative* importance of the input segment decreases.[3]

A second formulation with direct evolutional implication is that the instinctual drives "have led the nervous system . . .

3 The controversy "central versus peripheral" extends also to the problem "central versus peripheral selectivity of perception." It may be pertinent at this point to mention the work of Granit (1955) and others who found efferent centrifugal fibers in most sensory organs.

to its present high level of development," and, finally, that the "instincts [instinctual drives] may be the precipitates of the effects of external stimulation."[4]

Evolutional development repeats itself to a certain degree during ontogenesis and results in the process of internalization (Hartmann, 1939, 1950).

The evolutional development of the instinctual drives is paralleled by the transition from what Schneirla (1957) calls a biophysiological to a biopsychological organism. This development is implied in Freud's description of the development of the mental apparatus in Chapter VII of *The Interpretation of Dreams* (1900).

Freud's work is replete with other, more specific, phylogenetic formulations, mostly stated in terms of neo-Lamarckian theory, to which Freud stubbornly adhered throughout his life; e.g., the attribution of the oedipus complex to the inheritance of acquired characteristics (1913a, 1923, 1924b, 1939), or the assertion that the archaic heritage manifests itself in dream symbolism (1940).

This applies even more to Freud's speculations about the phylogenetic development of the id in relation to the superego. He was already grappling with this problem as early as in *Totem and Taboo* (1913a), but more particularly in *The Ego and the Id* (1923, pp. 36-39), and later in *Moses* (1939).

We can see that Freud's dilemma was based on two conceptions: (1) that the id "inherits" the oedipus complex[5] and thereby also becomes the core of the superego; and (2) that only the id can carry genetic information. While in "Analysis Terminable and Interminable" (1937) Freud spoke about in-

---

4 It is beyond the scope of this paper to discuss these last two formulations in terms of modern genetics. However, they can be reformulated in terms of selective evolution (L. Ritvo, 1965; Schur and Ritvo, 1966).

5 Even if modern geneticists are now thinking—albeit in a much more sophisticated way—about how the "genetic substance" can be changed, it would be difficult to formulate these ideas of Freud's in modern evolutionary terms.

nate aspects of ego development (see Hartmann, 1939), he stated in the *Outline* (1940) that the id, phylogenetically and ontogenetically the *"oldest"* portion of the mental apparatus, "contains everything that is inherited, that is present at birth, that is laid down in the constitution" (p. 145).

## THE ONTOGENESIS OF THE ID

The assumption of the "innate character" of the id was in line with phylogenetic formulations. It is in this area, however, that we again encounter a number of ambiguities in Freud's statements. We can trace these ambiguities to the following (overlapping) factors: (a) the historical development of Freud's formulations; (b) Freud's basically pragmatic approach. His formulations started with observation, while his theory had to start "from scratch." He was, therefore, ready to reformulate his conceptual framework whenever his observations necessitated such changes.

At different times in the development of his ideas, Freud assigned different weight to the relative role of "nature versus nurture," of "the innate versus the experiential," a factor which led to the ambiguities previously mentioned. His self analysis and analytic observations of patients led Freud to the discovery that sexuality begins in earliest infancy; this factor, in turn, induced him to conclude that the instinctual drives are innate givens, a formulation which very soon went beyond the aspect of seeing constitution as the main etiological factor in neurosogenesis. The instinctual drives and their vicissitudes were now conceived as the main motivating force in human behavior. The formulation of the libido theory and the concept of narcissism as well as the development of the structural theory were paralleled by the development of the dual instinct theory and the assumption of an innate endowment in terms of "Eros and Thanatos," or, as we would

[ 55 ]

prefer to say, libidinal and aggressive instinctual drives, with the implication that these drives are present *ab ovo*.

While Freud thus abandoned his *exaggerated* environmentalistic formulations and turned toward all aspects of internalization, he never lost sight of the influence of the environment on the development of mental functioning. Freud was a biologist, steeped in embryology, and was fully aware that Anlage cannot be more than a directional *Grundplan* (von Uexküll, 1934), that the mental apparatus, and along with it all mental functioning, develops as the result of interaction between an innate Anlage and experiential, ecological factors (in Hartmann's terms, the "average expectable environment"). Freud's concept of the complementary series was formulated with regard to this problem (1905c). Freud used this concept in connection with the same problem, "the innate versus the experiential," many times.

In a letter addressed to Else Voigtländer on October 1, 1911, Freud said:

> You suggest that I overestimate the importance of accidental influences on character formation and in contrast you stress the importance of constitutional factors, of disposition, which selects from among the experiences and allows them to become significant. Everything you say on this subject is excellent, except that its polemical application seems to be based on a misunderstanding. For, with a minor modification, we say the same.
>
> We find in psychoanalysis that we are dealing not with *one* disposition but with an infinite number of dispositions which are developed and fixed by accidental fate. The disposition is so to speak polymorphous. We also believe that this is again a case in which scientifically thinking people distort a cooperation into an antithesis. The question as to which is of greater significance, constitution or experience, which of the two elements decides character, can in my opinion only be answered by saying that δαίμων καὶ τύχη[6]

6 Titles of the first two stanzas of Goethe's poem "Urworte, Orphisch."

[fate and chance] and not one *or* the other are decisive. Why should there be an antithesis, since constitution after all is nothing but the sediment of experiences from a long line of ancestors; and why should the *individual* experience not be granted a share alongside the experience of ancestors?

Now, it seems that in single cases all these possibilities of variation are realized in such a way that in each individual sometimes this, sometimes that part of the inherited disposition becomes so dominating that it chooses some experiences and rejects others, whereas on the other hand accidental influences work here and there so powerfully that they arouse and fix this or that part of the originally dormant disposition.

If in our analytical work we concentrate more on the accidental influences than on the constitutional factors, we do so for two reasons. First, because the former have been overlooked and now have to be proved, whereas the latter are only too readily admitted; second, because on the basis of our experience we know something about the former, while about the latter we know as little as—nonanalysts. This predilection for the accidental, however, by no means signifies a denial of the constitutional. We are inclined more toward overdetermination and less toward antithesis than other observers.

We are also of the opinion that by appreciating the importance of the accidental we have taken the right road toward the understanding of constitution. It is the correct line of procedure. What remains inexplicable after a study of the accidental may be put down to constitution [1960, pp. 284-285].

Apart from general formulations of this kind, Freud discussed such matters as the interplay between "phylogenetic and ontogenetic" (innate and experiential) in the specific process of the dissolution of the oedipus complex (1924b). His claim, that the oedipus complex must "go to its destruction from its lack of success, from the effects of its internal impossibility" (p. 173), represented an emphasis on the experiential factors, stemming from clinical observation. He also said:

> Another view is that the Oedipus complex must collapse because the time has come for its disintegration, just as the milk-teeth fall out when the permanent ones begin to grow. Although the majority of human beings go through the Oedipus complex as an individual experience, it is nevertheless a phenomenon which is determined and laid down by heredity and which is bound to pass away according to programme when the next pre-ordained phase of development sets in [pp. 173-174].

This statement represents the phylogenetic, theoretical point of view. However, Freud continued:

> The justice of both these views cannot be disputed. Moreover, they are compatible. There is room for the ontogenetic view side by side with the more far-reaching phylogenetic one. It is also true that even at birth the whole individual is destined to die, and perhaps his organic disposition may already contain the indication of what he is to die from. Nevertheless, it remains of interest to follow out how this innate programme is carried out and in what way accidental noxae exploit his disposition [p. 174].

We can here substitute experience for the word "noxae."

Freud's pragmatic approach is exemplified by his description of the ontogenetic vicissitudes of infantile sexuality, resulting in the subsequent formulation of the phases of psychosexual development. The concept of the component instinctual drives was related to the maturation of the structural and functional development of various organ systems.

How does all this apply to the ontogenesis of the id?

Let us again turn to one sentence of a previously quoted paragraph from the *Outline:* [the id] "contains everything[7]

---

[7] This statement contradicts Freud's assumption (1937) of innate determinants of the ego.

that is inherited, that is *present at birth,* that is laid down in the constitution" (1940, p. 145; my italics).

On the one hand, this merely repeats some of Freud's formulations about the innate character of the instinctual drives; on the other hand, the clause "that is present at birth," corroborated by such formulations as "Originally . . . everything was id" (1940, p. 163), goes beyond this. They imply that the id is preformed, and as such is present *ab ovo.*

We could brush such statements off, attributing them to "loose formulations," if they were not also in line with the proposition that under the influence of exigencies from the external world one part of the id undergoes "a special development" to become the ego.

Other propositions in line with the assumption that the id is present at birth are those originally formulated in Freud's discussion of the "system *Ucs.,*" but later applied to the structure id: that the id and its "content" (*"Ucs."*) are "virtually immortal" (1933, p. 74), that the unconscious wishes "share this character of indestructibility with all other mental acts which are truly unconscious. . . . These are paths which have been laid down once and for all, which never fall into disuse and which, whenever an unconscious excitation recathects them, are always ready to conduct the excitatory process to discharge" (1900, p. 553).

When Freud spoke about the instinctual drives, he always emphasized their rigidity and conservative character.

We see, therefore, that one set of *theoretical* formulations implies that the id is present at birth, is conservative, immutable, indestructible.

The *pragmatic* formulations based on observation are quite different, however. As already mentioned, the psychosexual development from the oral to the genital organizations is always described in terms of *development* of the instinctual drives. These pragmatic developmental formulations are also

[ 59 ]

applied to the structure id. But there are additional genetic formulations, also based on observation, which again stem in part from the "topographic era."

1. We know that Freud at various times used the concept *Ucs.* in a "descriptive" (qualitative), "dynamic" sense, as well as in terms of a "system" (Freud, 1915a, 1923; Strachey, 1961; Gill, 1963). He made genetic formulations about the "system *Ucs.*," distinguishing between a "core" of the system which remained immutable and "immortal," and the "repressed," which was not always unconscious, and which under certain conditions (dreams, symptom formation, analysis) could again become conscious.[8]

Freud made similar genetic and "qualitative" distinctions between several "layers" of the structure id. In the *Outline* (1940) he said:

> The sole prevailing quality in the id is that of being unconscious. Id and unconscious are as intimately linked as ego and preconscious: indeed, in the former case the connection is even more exclusive. If we look back at the developmental history of an individual and of his psychical apparatus, we shall be able to perceive an important distinction in the id. Originally, to be sure, everything was id; the ego was developed out of the id by the continual influence of the external world. In the course of this slow development certain of the contents of the id were transformed into the preconscious state and so taken into the ego; others of its contents remained in the id unchanged, as its scarcely accessible nucleus. During this development, however, the young and feeble ego put back into the unconscious state some of the material it had already taken in, dropped it, and behaved in the same way to some fresh impressions which it *might* have taken in, so that these,

[8] The formulations concerning the "system preconscious" will not be discussed here. For different approaches, see Kris (1950), Eissler (1962), Arlow and Brenner (1964).

[ 60 ]

having been rejected, could leave a trace only in the id. In consideration of its origin we speak of this latter portion of the id as *the repressed*. It is of little importance that we are not always able to draw a sharp line between these two categories of contents of the id. They coincide approximately with the distinction between what was innately present originally and what was acquired in the course of the ego's development [p. 163].

2. The concept *regression,* which Freud also arrived at from observation, is the second genetic formulation applied to the structure id. I need not emphasize here the crucial importance of this concept for both theory and practice.

Besides these pragmatic formulations, we find in the *Outline* another, somewhat cryptic one, which is quite different from those previously quoted:

> We may picture an initial state as one in which the total available energy of Eros, which henceforward we shall speak of as 'libido', is present in the still *undifferentiated ego-id* and serves to neutralize the destructive tendencies which are simultaneously present [1940, pp. 149-150; my italics].

Here Freud was saying that at the beginning there was the energy of libido and of aggression. The structures id and ego developed later. Out of a cryptic, seemingly contradictory remark grew the heuristically fruitful concept of an undifferentiated phase (Hartmann, 1939; Hartmann, Kris, and Loewenstein, 1946).

To summarize the ambiguities in the theoretical formulations:

On the one hand, Freud assumed that the id was present at birth and immutable; that it contained all that was inherited. On the other hand, he also described it as undergoing maturational (sexual phase) and developmental changes (addition of "the repressed").[9]

Generally speaking, we can detect the following trend in Freud's formulations, a trend which in turn was in line with the historical development of the concept: upon the discovery of the intrinsic-innate determinants of mental functioning, these elements were mainly assigned to the id. The experiential, developmental formulations were expressed in connection with the concept ego. I might mention here, however, a thought recently expressed by Benjamin (1961) to the effect that Freud, despite what he called his "momentous error" (1950)—brought home to him by the discovery of the untruthfulness of his patients—was always impressed by the role of experiential factors in normal and abnormal development. On the one hand he thus made formulations and assumptions about the universality of certain innate givens, while on the other he displaced to a certain extent the role of highly specific experience from the ontogenetic to the phylogenetic domain. If the innate was *also* a precipitate of the historical experiential, then the distinction between innate and experiential became less crucial. Benjamin speculates that this reasoning may be an explanation of Freud's lifelong adherence to neo-Lamarckian views on heredity.[10]

It is by now a truism that we can find many later formulations by Freud (and others) which were at least alluded to in much earlier works. In all metapsychological studies we therefore turn automatically to Chapter VII of *The Interpretation of Dreams,* where we find formulations which, if applied consistently, might dispel some of the ambiguities.

Before undertaking this discussion, I shall cite some state-

[9] Nothing was said about the maturational and developmental aspects of the aggressive elements.

[10] Other possible reasons for this remarkable paradox are discussed in a later publication (Schur and Ritvo, 1966). See also Andersson (1962).

ments which other authors made concerning the development of the id.

Anna Freud (1936), for instance, said:

A man's id remains much the same throughout life. It is true that the instinctual impulses are capable of transformation when they come into collision with the ego and the demands of the outside world. But within the id itself little or no change takes place, *apart from the advance made from* pre-genital to genital instinctual aims [1936, pp. 152-153; my italics].

Hartmann (1939, 1952) and Hartmann, Kris, and Loewenstein (1946) have dealt extensively with the problem of the maturation and development of mental structures. Their main attention, however, for very obvious and valid reasons, has been directed toward ego development. Nevertheless, in discussing the functions of the id, these authors also speak of "the instinctual *tendencies* and their mental representatives" (1946, p. 31). Hartmann, describing the earliest phases of "differentiation" (from the undifferentiated phase), stated: "it is difficult to disentangle the nuclei of functions that will later serve the ego from those that we shall attribute to the id. Also, it is often hard to decide what part of it could already be described in terms of mental functioning . . . what the state of the id is at that level is unknown" (1952, p. 166). However, Hartmann also emphasized: (1) those changes in the id which are brought about by the *growth or development* of the instinctual drives through all their subsequent phases; (2) the modifications which, via the ego, analysis can induce in the id; (3) the id aspect of the outcome of repression (using as an example the dissolution of the oedipus complex); (4) and, by contrast, "the stubborn opposition to change of the instinctual drives" (1952).

# 7

## The Development of the "Wish"

I INDICATED earlier that Chapter VII of *The Interpretation of Dreams* contains certain genetic formulations that are relevant to a conceptualization of the structure id—thirty-three years before Freud worked out his structural theory. What I have in mind specifically are Freud's genetic formulations about the concept "wish." Freud arrived at these within the framework of what he called "our schematic picture of the psychical apparatus" (1900, p. 565).[1]

The very first sentence can be understood in both evolutional and ontogenetic terms: "There can be no doubt that that apparatus [too—*auch*] has only reached its present perfection after a long period of development" (p. 565).

Both genetic aspects were expressed in the next sentence: ". . . its first structure followed the plan of a reflex apparatus, so that any sensory excitation impinging on it could be promptly discharged along a motor path. But the exigencies of life interfere with this simple function, and it is to them, too, that the apparatus owes the impetus to further development."

Phylogenetically speaking, this formulation expresses in an extremely condensed fashion the development from the primitive forms of life whose functions are dictated on the

[1] Freud had made similar statements as early as in the "Project" (1895), and he repeated them later, with various modifications, e.g., in *Beyond the Pleasure Principle* (1920).

[ 64 ]

one hand by their genetic *Grundplan* (von Uexküll), while on the other hand they are overwhelmingly dependent on *external* stimulation. Every animal has an inborn tendency to respond to specific sensory stimulation, either by approach or by withdrawal (Schneirla, 1959). Any reaction to stimuli is species specific, and is determined also by the intensity of the stimuli. One can detect throughout evolution that, basically, stimuli of low intensity stimulate approach, while intense stimuli will result in withdrawal. What constitutes a low or intense stimulus is partly species specific and partly dependent on ontogenetic development. The maximal dependency on external stimulation has undergone the following changes in the course of evolution: paralleled by evolutional development of a more complex central nervous system, of the sympathetic systems, and of the endocrine and enzyme systems, the effect of external stimulation on behavior has become increasingly dependent on changes in the *milieu intérieur* (inner environment). While the function of various organ systems still remains partly dependent on external physical stimuli (temperature, light, etc.), inner change determines both spontaneous behavior and the response to external stimulation.

The ontogenetic aspect of Freud's formulation implies that the primitive mental apparatus of the newborn infant follows the plan of a reflex apparatus. At this stage the newborn infant's equipment and functioning correspond to the early evolutional stages described in the previous paragraphs. Changes in the *milieu intérieur* (homeostatic disequilibrium) influence the infant's behavior and, more specifically, the use of such inborn apparatuses, which guarantee survival through the gratification of physiological needs. These *inner* changes also influence the infant's responsiveness to *external* stimulation, e.g., by contact with the nipple, to which it responds with the species-specific pattern of rooting and sucking.[2] It is from this level that the mental apparatus must proceed to its eventual "perfection."

The progression from the simple reflex to what Freud called a wish—and beyond that to fantasies, etc.—also has its phylogenetic and ontogenetic implications.

Schneirla (1957, 1959) has described the evolutional development from "biosocial" to "psychosocial" patterns, from "approach" and "withdrawal," which are biophysiological concepts, to "seeking" and "avoidance," which are biopsychological concepts.

Ontogenetically, the progression from a *reflex* to a *wish*—mediated by a change in the infant's inner environment, the availability of an average expectable environment, and the presence of species-specific executive (primary autonomous [Hartmann, 1939, 1950, 1958]) apparatuses—is the function of maturation and development.

[2] This schematic presentation is not intended to minimize the importance of the variegated external stimuli which impinge on the infant (see Wolff, 1959). For a discussion of what is "external" at an early phase of development, see Chapter 8.

# 8

## Maturational and Developmental Factors of the Id

THE CONCEPT maturation does not imply merely a process of structural and functional growth under specific genetic determinants. Maturation connotes growth *and* differentiation, both of which, from a very early age, are also dependent to a certain degree on all the stimulative influences impinging on the maturing organism from its environment.

Development is therefore a process of constant interaction among innate, maturational, and experiential factors (Schneirla, 1957; Spitz, 1959). The range, the tempo, and the over-all direction of development are species specific. For example, the innate endowment of man predestines him—given an average expectable environment—to go through the process of what Hartmann calls internalization and the parallel development of mental structures. The best example of these is the development of the memory apparatus and of thought processes.

An important feature of development is the self-propelling stimulation which is operative at every stage of maturation. The tempo and range of development will depend on the ability to integrate neurally the results of such maturation.

We must keep in mind that these aspects of development, which biopsychologists call "spiral," result not only in an "improvement" of function but in what we usually refer to as a hierarchical development (Spitz, 1959).

[ 67 ]

Let us now return to Freud's formulation of the development of a wish. He describes the transition from a reflex action as follows:

> The excitations produced by internal needs seek discharge. . . . But the situation remains unaltered, for the excitation arising from an internal need is not due to a force producing a *momentary* impact but to one which is in continuous operation. A change can only come about if . . . an 'experience of satisfaction' can be achieved which puts an end to the internal stimulus [1900, p. 565].

What follows is the crucial developmental formulation:

> An essential component of this experience of satisfaction is a particular perception (that of nourishment, in our example) the mnemic image of which remains associated thenceforward with the memory trace of the excitation produced by the need. As a result of the link that has thus been established, next time this need arises a psychical impulse will at once emerge which will seek to re-cathect the mnemic image of the perception and to re-evoke the perception itself, that is to say, to re-establish the situation of the original satisfaction. An impulse of this kind is what we call a wish; the reappearance of the perception is the fulfilment of the wish. . . . Thus the aim of this *first psychical activity* was to produce a 'perceptual identity'[1]—a repetition of the perception which was linked with the satisfaction of the need.
> [1] [I.e. something perceptually identical with the 'experience of satisfaction'.] [1900, pp. 565-566; my italics.]

I have indicated in previous publications (1958, 1960a, 1961a) that the emergence of the "wish" marks the beginning of the functioning of what we call psychic structure. I have also stressed the difference between the physiological concept "need" and the psychological concept "wish." *I propose that this transition from functioning on the level of a reflex ap-*

*paratus to that of a wish represents the developmental model for the transition from "somatic needs" to instinctual drives as mental representations of stimuli arising within the soma, and for the development of the structure id from the undifferentiated phase.* This proposition, which is in line with Freud's definition of instinctual drives as mental representations, must assume that the development of the id makes use of certain—albeit primitive—perceptions and memory traces.

As I have mentioned earlier in Chapter 3, such an assumption seems ambiguous, because both perception and memory are considered to be ego functions. Some developmental considerations, both phylogenetic and ontogenetic, are in order here. We must always remind ourselves that the organism starts at birth with an Anlage and with certain apparatuses. Hartmann, who has taught us the importance of such innate apparatuses, traced their development mainly from the vantage point of ego development. *Nothing prevents us from assuming, however, that what we call the id also uses such innate apparatuses in its development.*[1] A similar argument is implied in Gill's suggestion (1963) that the apparatus *Cs.* is at the disposal of all psychic structures. This assumption is inherent in the following concepts:

1. The concept of an undifferentiated phase involves the assumption that the id is a product of development.

---

[1] This formulation has on the one hand found confirmation in recent research on sleep and dreaming and on the other hand has contributed to a possible explanation of the fact that the stage 1 of rapid eye movement periods is present at birth, at a time when, as Fisher (1965) says, "it is inconceivable that dreaming is taking place because psychic structure has not yet developed" (p. 272). Concurring with statements of mine, Fisher states: "we cannot speak of instinctual drives until psychic structure develops, until the formation of the 'wish,' that is, when memory traces of experiences of gratification and frustration are laid down. . . . I would like to stress that dreaming as a psychic event also cannot occur until the emergence of the 'wish,' until psychic structure formation advances to the point of memory trace development of sufficient stability that traces of past events can be aroused to hallucinatory intensity during dreaming sleep" (p. 273).

2. Development—as discussed previously—is not simply based on the unfolding of an Anlage, but is the result of interaction between innate, maturational, and experiential factors.

We can now come back to Freud's previously quoted statement that "the id has its own world of perception" (1940). *We might prefer to say that the id uses a special kind of perception and percept in a special way.*

If we assume that the id is subject to development and that it utilizes some percepts and memory traces, we must also postulate an interaction between the *development* of the id and the *development* of perception and memory. Such interaction has been studied mainly in relation to early ego development.

In discussing the development of perception as applied to the development of the id, it might be pertinent to indicate briefly the following facts gained from a comparative study of the evolution of perception at different phyletic levels.

1. Irritability or sensitivity to stimulation is common to all living matter. The term perception should be restricted, however, to some capacity for *organizing* sensory data.

2. The capacity to organize sensory data differs at various phyletic levels. Such differences are not only quantitative but qualitative.

3. The ability to progress from the lowest functional order to organized perception is species specific. There is, however, no direct correlation between the initial rate of maturational development of perception and the final level it achieves in ontogeny. As a matter of fact, we know that—in contrast to much more advanced mammals and especially primates—lower vertebrates, such as birds, achieve a discrimination of percepts within a short time after hatching but do not progress beyond this level to any appreciable extent.

Jacobsen et al. (1953) have found, for example, that chimpanzees are well ahead of human infants during the first nine months, but are then overtaken rapidly in conceptual accomplishment and concept formation (see Schneirla, 1957; Piaget, 1936; Hebb, 1949).

The following facts pertaining to the innate equipment and early development of the infant are pertinent at this point:

1. The homeostatic equilibrium of the newborn infant is still extremely labile. While homeostasis as a physiological regulative principle applies to all animals, the complexity of this principle and of the apparatus (using this term in its widest form) engaged in its realization grows progressively in the phyletic series. At birth this growth and maturation are not yet complete.

2. The infant's behavior indicates a low threshold of response to some kinds of perception of stimuli originating in its interior (Freud, 1940, p. 198). This has also been expressed in other terms: namely, that the stimulus barrier to perceptions originating from within has a low threshold in infancy (Schur, 1962).

3. By contrast, the threshold against stimuli originating from without is relatively much higher. This discrepancy is due to a lag in the development of the central nervous system.[2]

4. Maturation tends to progress in a cephalocaudal direction (Greenacre, 1960; Rangell, 1963). It seems legitimate to assume that this applies not only to the neuromuscular patterning but also to the sensory equipment, and therefore to the delicate interplay of sensorimotor function, especially of the snout area (lips and the oral cavity).

5. Every stage of maturation and development has a self-

[2] It might therefore not be semantically quite correct to speak of a lack of cathexis of peripheral perception at this stage of development. See also Benjamin's important discussion (1961).

propelling quality which results in a spiraling effect in sensorimotor perception.

I postulate that all these factors, including the primary autonomous apparatuses, which are recognized to have such an important bearing on the early development of ego structures, also contribute to the development of the id out of the undifferentiated phase.

If the wish to establish a perceptual identity (i.e., "something perceptually identical with 'the experience of satisfaction' ") is, so to speak, the functional prototype of the id, then it stands to reason to assume that the complexity of this experience of satisfaction will increase with the range of sensorimotor perception and the simultaneous development of neural trace effects.

As applied to the model of the hungry infant (Rapaport, 1951a), we may assume the following developmental steps:

1. The very first experiences of satisfaction arise under circumstances of change in the homeostatic equilibrium which probably sensitize the infant and make him more susceptible to using his two vitally important apparatuses for "approach"—the rooting and sucking reflexes—whenever an adequate stimulus is provided.

Even this stage of development is somewhat more complex than the one Freud described as following the plan of a reflex apparatus, because the "reflex" is brought into play *both* by a change of the inner state *and* by an external stimulus. In Freud's formulation both factors impinge on the primitive mental apparatus from the outside (of the apparatus).[3]

2. We can now assume two parallel developments: the maturational development of the sensorimotor apparatus of

[3] We may already state here, however, that at this stage there is no distinction between stimuli originating from outside the organism and those originating from within it. Both are "outside of the mental apparatus" (see Chapter 12).

the snout region, along with tactile, taste, olfactory, and auditory perceptions; and the development of memory traces of these percepts.

In this complex network of percept and memory traces there must also be included the registration of experiences of satisfaction (tension reduction), which contrasts with the registration of homeostatic disequilibrium (tension). Psychoanalytic theory assumes that this pair of experiences becomes representative of the whole set of underlying networks of percepts and memory traces, which are linked together by firmly fixed associations.

3. We can assume that the reciprocal stimulation of maturational and experiential factors will result in increasing complexity of mental representations of needs and their modes of gratification. The source of both stimuli and gratification will at first gain mental representation in a more global sense.

We recognize that the differential between tension and tension-reduction experiences through satisfaction of oral needs has a greater valence at early stages than the perception of other sensory stimuli (cutaneous, olfactory, thermic, visual, auditory, equilibrium, etc.)—notwithstanding the vital contributions of the latter to the total development. We assume that these can be perceived in a discriminating way only at a later stage of development (see also Piaget, 1936; Wolff, 1960; Spitz, 1965).

4. We can further assume that certain perceptions, including those of external stimuli, which *precede* the final satisfaction and are essential for the execution of the "wish" (instinctual drive discharge), will also become part of this network of percepts and memory traces. The sequence—rooting, perception of the nipple, sucking, tension reduction—is paradigmatic for this inclusion of an external stimulus.

This sequence subsumes the behavioral elements which

ethologists have conceptualized as "appetitive behavior" *and* the consummatory act (Lorenz, 1937; Tinbergen, 1951; Thorpe, 1956; for a discussion see also Rapaport, 1960a). We may assume that the *whole sequence* which is initiated by the instinctual drives, as well as all the aspects of appetitive behavior, can become part of the wish.

We must remind ourselves that the concept of instinctual drives, especially as formulated in Freud's later works (1920, 1923, 1924a, 1933, 1940), encompasses far more than the original formulations (1900) which were based on the model of the hungry infant seeking oral gratification (see Rapaport, 1951a).

All the percepts of various stimuli enumerated in my discussion of the third step in the development of the wish, as well as their mental representations, eventually become cathected by instinctual drive energy. The observations of Wolff (1959) on newborn infants show that their responsiveness to moving sounds and visual objects starts during the first days of life.[4] This responsiveness is limited to the time when they are *not* in a state indicating physiological stress.

With the development of instinctual drives as mental representations of somatic needs and wishes, an analogous observation can be made. In the absence of urgent instinctual needs, functions other than those leading to consummatory acts which relieve acute distress can become cathected, and all such functions can be included in the wish.

It is pertinent to point out here that Piaget (1936) made most of his observations during periods of relative absence of urgent instinctual demands. It is obvious that these considerations are important for such problems as play, forepleasure, the investment of ego functions with instinctual drive ca-

---

4 See also the observations made by Lustman (1956) on the neonate's early responsiveness to stimulation of the skin.

thexis, for the understanding of the affect pleasure. These, however, are beyond the scope of this monograph (see Hartmann, 1939, 1947, 1950, 1955; Rapaport, 1957, 1960a; White, 1959, 1963).

In this discussion of the development of the "wish" as an essential part of what I consider to be the development of the id I have tried to put into proper perspective the intricate interplay between the physiological needs, the "pressure" exerted by the maturation of the central nervous system and the autonomous apparatuses, in interaction with the environment. This interaction provides both a re-establishment of homeostatic equilibrium, which cannot be achieved by inner regulation, and such stimuli as are essential for the development of both id and ego.

My developmental conceptualizations of the id are in line with the assumption that all mental manifestations are dependent on *growth and maturation*. This was the pivotal assumption in Freud's theory of the psychosexual development (1905c). The concept of the component instinctual drives (oral, anal, phallic) was based on this assumption as well. That the id is subject to developmental processes has also been assumed by Anna Freud (1936), Hartmann (1952), Hartmann, Kris, and Loewenstein (1946), and others, as was mentioned in Chapter 6.

If we assume, as previously discussed, that the id is "supplied" by "somatic" (physiological) sources, percepts and memory traces, and "the repressed," there is reason to assume, too, that the id undergoes changes even beyond the organization of the genital phase. If we think of psychic structures in terms of a continuum, if we assume that the id—and its "functional unit," the wish—has a content, if we subscribe to Freud's hypothesis of the dynamic unconscious, then it becomes artificial to draw a strict dividing line between a certain state of psychic energy and an unconscious wish, and to apportion the latter to the ego.[5]

Moreover, these developmental formulations are in line not only with those of "classical" psychoanalysis (including, of course, ego psychology) but also with the formulations of biology and with the work of such representatives of developmental psychology as Piaget (1936), Schneirla (1957), and Werner (1948). (See also Rapaport, 1957, 1960a; Wolff, 1960.)

I assume that this development is a continuing process which remains dependent on physiological needs, their mental representations, the object world, and the state of the apparatus of perception and execution. It will follow the model of the first wishes. It is conceivable or even probable, however, that the development of wishes representing the gratification of the aggressive instinctual drive takes a somewhat different form. We know less about this, partly because it is more difficult to conceptualize the percepts and memory traces underlying such wishes, and partly because we can observe the manifestations of the aggressive instinctual drives only in connection with those of the libidinal ones.[6]

In the preceding chapters I have discussed the various definitions of the id, its functions, its genetic aspect, its relationship to the instinctual drives, the concept "wish," which I described as the functional unit of the id, and its development. Other concepts which are integral to the concept id are the primary process and the pleasure and unpleasure principles.

[5] This latter development is also tacitly assumed, e.g., by Beres (1962), who would prefer, however, to restrict the concept id to an energy (economic) concept. The perception and memory traces of need gratification are based on growth, maturation, *and* development. This development is also dependent on an interaction with the environment (object), which therefore also contributes to the development of the id.

[6] I may add here that it might be useful, at least heuristically, to assume a development of libidinal and aggressive energy from an undifferentiated ("physiological") energy; such a development would parallel the development of psychic structures from the undifferentiated phase (Fenichel, 1945; Jacobson, 1953; Rapaport, 1957, 1960b; Schur, 1958; Loewenstein, 1965).

# 9

## The Primary Process

IT IS GENERALLY conceded that what is called the "primary process" is an essential characteristic of the id. The concept primary process has been considered basic to psychoanalytic theory since Freud first formulated it in 1900, subsuming under it most of the characteristics of what he then called the "system *Ucs.*" (alternately the "primary system"; see quotation below) and later occasionally the "dynamic unconscious,"[1] prior to eventually formulating the structural point of view.

The concept primary process has shared the fate of so many other psychoanalytic concepts in that it has not been uniformly used in the psychoanalytic literature. Unlike the case of other theoretical concepts, however, this was not due to any significant changes made by Freud in his original formulations concerning the primary process. In fact, Freud's *over-all* formulations remained uniform, from *The Interpretation of Dreams* (1900) to the *Outline* (1940).

However, as we shall see shortly, the concept primary process encompasses so many aspects of mental functioning that, without changing the basic formulation, Freud used it differently in different works, depending on the aspects of his over-all concept he wished to emphasize.

Freud had already *described* the mental processes which he was eventually to subsume under the term "primary

---

1 For an exhaustive discussion of these concepts, see Gill (1963).

[ 77 ]

process" in Chapter VI of *The Interpretation of Dreams*, which deals with the dream work (1900, p. 277). His first *formulation* of the term "primary process" in Chapter VII of that work indicated the various contexts in which he would thenceforth use the term.

As a result of the unpleasure principle, then, the first $\psi$-system is totally incapable of bringing anything disagreeable into the context of its *thoughts* [my italics]. It is unable to do anything but wish. If things remained at that point, the thought-activity of the second system would be obstructed, since it requires free access to *all* the memories laid down by experience. Two possibilities now present themselves. Either the activity of the second system might set itself entirely free from the unpleasure principle and proceed without troubling about the unpleasure of memories; or it might find a method of cathecting unpleasurable memories which would enable it to avoid releasing the unpleasure. We may dismiss the first of these possibilities, for the unpleasure principle clearly regulates the course of excitation in the second system as much as in the first. We are consequently left with the remaining possibility that the second system cathects memories in such a way that there is an inhibition of their discharge, including, therefore, an inhibition of discharge (comparable to that of a motor innervation) in the direction of the development of unpleasure. We have therefore been led from two directions to the hypothesis that cathexis by the second system implies a simultaneous inhibition of the discharge of excitation; we have been led to it by regard for the unpleasure principle and also . . . by the principle of the least expenditure of innervation. Let us bear this firmly in mind, for it is the key to the whole theory of repression: *the second system can only cathect an idea if it is in a position to inhibit any development of unpleasure that may proceed from it.* Anything that could evade that inhibition would be inaccessible to the second system as well as to the first; for it would promptly be dropped in obedience to the unpleasure principle. The inhibition of unpleasure need

[ 78 ]

not, however, be a complete one: a beginning of it must be allowed, since that is what informs the second system of the nature of the memory concerned and of its possible unsuitability for the purpose which the thought-process has in view.

I propose to describe the psychical process of which the first system alone admits as the 'primary process', and the process which results from the inhibition imposed by the second system as the 'secondary process'.

There is yet another reason for which, as I can show, the second system is obliged to correct the primary process. The primary process endeavours to bring about a discharge of excitation in order that, with the help of the amount of excitation thus accumulated, it may establish a 'perceptual identity' [with the experience of satisfaction (see pp. 565-6)]. The secondary process, however, has abandoned this intention and taken on another in its place—the establishment of a *thought* identity' [with that experience]. All thinking is no more than a circuitous path from the memory of a satisfaction (a memory which has been adopted as a purposive idea) to an identical cathexis of the same memory which it is hoped to attain once more through an intermediate stage of motor experiences. Thinking must concern itself with the connecting paths between ideas, without being led astray by the *intensities* of those ideas. But it is obvious that condensations of ideas, as well as intermediate and compromise structures, must obstruct the attainment of the identity aimed at. Since they substitute one idea for another, they cause a deviation from the path which would have led on from the first idea. Processes of this kind are therefore scrupulously avoided in secondary thinking. It is easy to see, too, that the unpleasure principle, which in other respects supplies the thought-process with its most important signposts, puts difficulties in its path towards establishing 'thought identity'. Accordingly, thinking must aim at freeing itself more and more from exclusive regulation by the unpleasure principle and at restricting the development of affect in thought-activity to the minimum required for acting as a signal. . . .

[ 79 ]

When I described one of the psychical processes occurring in the mental apparatus as the 'primary' one, what I had in mind was not merely considerations of relative importance and efficiency; I intended also to choose a name which would give an indication of its chronological priority. It is true that, so far as we know, no psychical apparatus exists which possesses a primary process only and that such an apparatus is to that extent a theoretical fiction. But this much is a fact: the primary processes are present in the mental apparatus from the first, while it is only during the course of life that the secondary processes unfold, and come to inhibit and overlay the primary ones; it may even be that their complete domination is not attained until the prime of life. In consequence of the belated appearance of the secondary processes, the core of our being, consisting of unconscious wishful impulses, remains inaccessible to the understanding and inhibition of the preconscious; the part played by the latter is restricted once and for all to directing along the most expedient paths the wishful impulses that arise from the unconscious. These unconscious wishes exercise a compelling force upon all later mental trends, a force which those trends are obliged to fall in with or which they may perhaps endeavour to divert and direct to higher aims. A further result of the belated appearance of the secondary process is that a wide sphere of mnemic material is inaccessible to preconscious cathexis.

Among these wishful impulses derived from infancy, which can neither be destroyed nor inhibited, there are some whose fulfilment would be a contradiction of the purposive ideas of secondary thinking. The fulfilment of these wishes would no longer generate an affect of pleasure but of unpleasure; and *it is precisely this transformation of affect which constitutes the essence of what we term 'repression'* [pp. 600-604].

Freud here distinguished clearly between two $\psi$-systems and two types of mental processes—a primary and a secondary one. The distinction was made: (1) in terms of the unpleasure principle,[2] which in turn regulated the *"context of thoughts"* or the "psychical processes" prevailing within these two systems by way of repression; (2) in genetic terms, indicating that the primary mental processes were chronologically older than the secondary ones, arising at a much earlier phase in the development of the mental apparatus than the latter; (3) in adaptive, teleological terms,[3] which could be phrased in the following way: the establishment of a perceptual identity (of gratification) is the purpose of the primary system, while the establishment of a "thought identity" is the aim of the secondary process. Such an aim would be obstructed by "condensations of ideas."[4]

When Freud introduced the concept of condensation, to which he devoted an entire subchapter in the section on the dream work, he was trying to find a term which would illustrate the striking difference between the latent dream thoughts and the manifest dream content, which are

. . . like two versions of the same subject-matter in two different languages. Or, more properly, the dream-content seems like a transcript of the dream-thoughts into another mode of expression, whose characters and syntactic laws it is our business to discover by comparing the original and the translation. The dream-thoughts are immediately comprehensible, as soon as we have learnt them. The dream-content, on the other hand, is expressed as it were in a pictographic script, the characters of which have to be transposed individually into the language of the dream-thoughts [1900, p. 277].

Here we have the fact of 'compression' or 'condensation', which has become familiar in the dream-work. It is this that is mainly responsible for the bewildering impression made

2 For a detailed discussion, see Chapter 12.

3 In a forthcoming publication, Gill will deal with an application of all metapsychological points of view to the concept "primary process" (personal communication).

4 The aim of attaining "thought identity" was later extended to the necessity of cathecting "word representations" (1915c).

on us by dreams, for nothing at all analogous to it is known to us in mental life that is normal and accessible to consciousness [p. 595].

Thoughts which are mutually contradictory make no attempt to do away with each other, but persist side by side. They often combine to form condensations, just as though there were no contradiction between them, or arrive at compromises such as our conscious thoughts would never tolerate but such as are often admitted in our actions [p. 596].

The concept of condensation was meant to express more than this, however. It applied not only to the dream work but also, in one of its principal aspects, to that amazing process by which some, if not most, memory traces are stored in the "mental apparatus."[5] The process might be compared to that of producing an "ultra-microfilm" which simultaneously would record its material in a certain code that defied all laws of Aristotelian logic, but would nonetheless follow certain "rules" so that it could be deciphered by Freud with the aid of clues furnished by free association and a study of neurotic symptoms, dreams, parapraxes, and jokes. Fisher and his co-workers (1954, 1957; Fisher and Paul, 1959) have shown convincingly that percepts are turned into memory traces and stored in the mental apparatus in accordance with similar rules.

Freud, too, was convinced that there was a comparable elaboration of visual percepts, as we can see from an exchange of letters between him and Arnold Zweig, a contemporary German novelist, in September, 1930.[6]

[5] Some of the memory traces which are stored after being subjected to the process of condensation are relatively accessible to "re-expansion" into their original components, while others have to overcome various degrees of countercathectic forces (Fisher, 1954, 1957).

[6] I am grateful to the Sigmund Freud Copyright Ltd. and to Mr. Arnold Zweig for permission to quote from these letters.

Zweig had been suffering from an eye ailment involving changes in the

Other "methods" by means of which the dream work and the storage of certain memory traces took place were delineated by Freud, among others, as displacement, the suspension of the law of contradiction, the use of symbols, and the failure to distinguish between past and present, all of which were included as characteristics of the primary process. He had recognized by that time the analogy between processes of the dream work and mental processes operating in symptom formation. He said:

> . . . the chief characteristic of these processes is that the whole stress is laid upon making the cathecting energy mobile and capable of discharge; the content and the proper meaning of the psychical elements to which the cathexes are attached are treated as of little consequence. It might have been supposed that condensation and the formation of compromises is only carried out for the sake of facilitating repression, that is, when it is a question of transforming thoughts into images. But the analysis—and still more the synthesis—of dreams which include no such regression to images, e.g. the dream of 'Autodidasker' [pp. 298 ff.], exhibits the same processes of displacement and condensation as the rest. . . .
>
> One of these [psychical processes] produces perfectly rational dream-thoughts, of no less validity than normal thinking; while the other treats these thoughts in a manner which is in the highest degree bewildering and irrational. . . . It would not be possible for us to answer this question [about the origin of the dream work] if we had not made some headway in the study of the psychology of

---

cornea and leading to distorted vision. Zweig described quite vividly in a letter to Freud how such visual distortion was influencing what we might call his hypnagogic phenomena, which he subjected to a very insightful analysis. In his answer, after referring to the phenomenon of "crystal-gazing" (these two words in English in the original letter), and to the observations of Silberer (see Freud, 1900), Freud confirmed Zweig's assumptions, ending his letter with the remark: "Durch die Lücke in der Netzhaut sieht man tief hinein ins Ubw. . . ." ["Through the breach in the retina, one can look deep into the Ucs. . . ."]

the neuroses, and particularly of hysteria. We have found from this that the same irrational psychical processes, and others that we have not specified, dominate the production of hysterical symptoms. . . . If they [rational thoughts in hysteria] force themselves upon our notice at any point, we discover by analysing the symptom which has been produced that . . . normal thoughts have been submitted to abnormal treatment: *they have been transformed into the symptom by means of condensation and the formation of compromises, by way of superficial associations and in disregard of contradictions* . . . [1900, p. 597].

Freud ascribed *all* these characteristics to the thought processes ("mental processes"; "contents") of what he called successively the first $\psi$-system, the system *Ucs.*, the dynamic *Ucs.*, and eventually the structure id.

Freud was not satisfied merely with conceptualizing his *observations* on the working of these "mental processes" in the "first $\psi$-system," which he subsumed under the term primary process. He was always seeking *explanatory* formulations which might give us greater—though hypothetical—insight into the working of the mental apparatus. We have learned from the Fliess letters (1950) about some aspects of the development of Freud's hypotheses. In the "Project" Freud still attempted to find a neurophysiological model for the working of the mental apparatus. He subsequently abandoned this attempt, returning to it only once—apart from occasional passages (e.g., 1920, 1923)—thirty years later in his short paper "A Note upon the 'Mystic Writing-Pad'" (1925a). From 1900 on Freud tried, at least, to formulate his explanatory concepts in psychological terms. In *The Interpretation of Dreams* Freud extensively used as an explanatory concept what he was afterward (from 1915 on) to call the economic point of view, applying it to dream formation, to his basic model of the mental apparatus, and to his formulation of the constancy and unpleasure principles (see Chapters 11 and 12).

[ 84 ]

I speculated earlier about the reasons for the special emphasis Freud placed on economic formulations in his paper on "The Unconscious" (1915c) when I discussed his various definitions of the concept instinctual drives. Freud used the economic point of view as one of the main explanatory concepts of the primary process, attempting thereby to elucidate the following points:

1. The "primary $\psi$-system" can do nothing but wish (the same formulation was later applied to the id). We may add that these wishes press for immediate gratification. It is the "secondary $\psi$-system" which tries to establish "perceptual identity" by "a circuitous path" (1900, p. 602). In later formulations Freud declared that the secondary system accounted for the faculty of delay (1911b), of countercathexis and defense (1915b, 1915c, 1923, 1926). He expressed the tendency to and faculty of immediate gratification in economic terms when he stated that the primary system operated with free, uninhibited, "freely mobile" energy.[7] According to Freud, this state of (psychic) energy explained the possibility of "rapid drive discharge" essential to immediate gratification of a wish.

2. In Freud's view, the phenomena of condensation and displacement could also be explained by an easy shift of cathexis, which in turn presupposed a free, uninhibited flow of energy. This easy shift facilitated the special concentration of cathexes on certain mental contents, endowing these with a special "quality" of attracting attention cathexis. It is indicative of the multiple meanings which Freud assigned to the concept condensation, as well as to the concept primary process, that on the one hand he used economic formulations to *explain* the term condensation, and on the other hand stated

[7] For a discussion of the terminology, and more particularly certain contradictions in the use of the term "mobile energy" in the English translation of "free drive energy" and "neutral energy," applied, for example, to attention cathexis, see Gill (1963, pp. 13-14) and Chapter 3, footnote 4 of this monograph.

that the many "irrational" mental processes he described as characteristic of the primary process *aimed at a goal,* a goal that he in turn described in economic terms (see 1900, p. 597, a passage which I quoted earlier in this chapter).

It is my contention that the term "primary process" was conceived by Freud as a broader concept, characterizing the operation of the "primary ψ-system" (eventually called the id), and that the economic formulation was only an explanatory hypothesis intended to account for some of the mechanisms of that process, such as condensation and displacement.

I have already mentioned that Freud also used the term primary process in a genetic framework and with adaptive implications. It would require a systematic application of all metapsychological points of view to establish the full meaning of the concept primary process. It is therefore not surprising to find that throughout Freud's work his emphasis varied as he considered different aspects of this term. A number of quotations will illustrate this.

Freud's economic formulations concerning the activity of the two systems are contained in the following paragraphs:

In order to be able to employ the power of movement to make alterations in the external world that shall be effective, it is necessary to accumulate a great number of experiences in the mnemic systems and a multiplicity of permanent records of the associations called up in this mnemic material by different purposive ideas. . . . We can now carry our hypotheses a step further. The activity of this second system, constantly feeling its way, and alternately sending out and withdrawing cathexes, needs on the one hand to have the whole of the material of memory freely at its command; but on the other hand it would be an unnecessary expenditure of energy if it sent out large quantities of cathexis along the various paths of thought and thus caused them to drain away to no useful purpose and diminish the quantity available for altering the external world. I therefore postulate that for the sake of efficiency the second system succeeds in retaining the major part of its cathexes of energy in a state of quiescence and in employing only a small part on displacement. The mechanics of these processes are quite unknown to me; anyone who wished to take these ideas seriously would have to look for physical analogies to them and find a means of picturing the movements that accompany excitation of neurones. All that I insist upon is the idea that the activity of the *first* ψ-system is directed towards securing the *free discharge* of the quantities of excitation, while the *second* system, by means of the cathexes emanating from it, succeeds in *inhibiting* this discharge and in transforming the cathexis into a quiescent one, no doubt with a simultaneous raising of its potential. I presume, therefore, that under the dominion of the second system the discharge of excitation is governed by quite different mechanical conditions from those in force under the dominion of the first system [1900, p. 599].[8]

Here again Freud combined his economic concepts with a teleological, adaptive one.

In *The Psychopathology of Everyday Life* (1901) he compared the operation of the process of condensation in parapraxes with that in dreams.

. . . in my *Interpretation of Dreams* I have demonstrated the part played by the work of *condensation* in forming what is called the manifest dream-content out of the latent dream-thoughts. A similarity of any sort between two elements of the unconscious material—a similarity between the things themselves or between their verbal presentations —is taken as an opportunity for creating a third, which is a composite or compromise idea. In the dream-content this third element represents both its components; and it is as a consequence of its originating in this way that it so fre-

---

8 While Freud's economic formulations about psychic energy are generally couched in psychological terms (see above), they also clearly reflect his earlier neurophysiological orientation.

quently has various contradictory characteristics. The formation of substitutions and contaminations which occurs in slips of the tongue is accordingly a beginning of the work of condensation which we find taking a most vigorous share in the construction of dreams [pp. 58-59].

The mechanism of parapraxes and chance actions, as we have come to know it by our employment of analysis, can be seen to correspond in its most essential points with the mechanism of dream-formation which I have discussed in the chapter on the 'dream-work' in my *Interpretation of Dreams*. In both cases we find condensations and com-promise-formations (contaminations). We have the same situation: by unfamiliar paths, and by the way of external associations, unconscious thoughts find expression as modifications of other thoughts. The incongruities, absurdities and errors of the dream-content, which result in the dream being scarcely recognized as the product of psychical activity, originate in the same way, though it is true with a freer use of the means at hand, as our common mistakes in everyday life. In both cases *the appearance of an incorrect function is explained by the peculiar mutual interference between two or several correct functions* [1901, pp. 277-278].

In none of these examples of condensation, which is an essential mechanism of the primary process, did Freud find it necessary to use economic formulations. This applied also, for example, to Freud's use of the term condensation in the interpretation of Dora's first dream:

'Mother's jewel-case' was therefore introduced in two places in the dream; and this element replaced all mention of Dora's infantile jealousy, of the drops (that is, of the sexual wetness), of being dirtied by the discharge, and, on the other hand, of her present thoughts connected with the temptation—the thoughts which were urging her to reciprocate the man's love, and which depicted the sexual situation (alike desirable and menacing) that lay before her. The element of 'jewel case' was more than any other a product of condensation and displacement, and a compromise between contrary mental currents. The multiplicity of its origin—both from infantile and contemporary sources—is no doubt pointed to by its double appearance in the content of the dream [1905a, pp. 91-92].

When Freud compared "dream work" with "joke work" he again discussed the mechanisms characteristic of the primary process, as well as the dream work, the "system *Ucs.*," and the id, without resorting to economic terms.

The interesting processes of condensation accompanied by the formation of a substitute, which we have recognized as the core of the technique of verbal jokes, point towards the formation of dreams, in the mechanism of which the same psychical processes have been discovered. This is equally true, however, of the techniques of conceptual jokes —displacement, faulty reasoning, absurdity, indirect representation, representation by the opposite—which re-appear one and all in the technique of the dream-work. Displacement is responsible for the puzzling appearance of dreams, which prevents our recognizing that they are a continuation of our waking life. The use of absurdity and nonsense in dreams has cost them the dignity of being regarded as psychical products and has led the authorities to suppose that a disintegration of the mental activities and a cessation of criticism, morality and logic are necessary conditions of the formation of dreams. Representation by the opposite is so common in dreams that even the popular books of dream-interpretation, which are on a completely wrong tack, are in the habit of taking it into account. Indirect representation—the replacement of a dream-thought by an allusion, by something small, a symbolism akin to analogy —is precisely what distinguishes the mode of expression of dreams from that of our waking life [1905b, pp. 88-89].

This was true also in the discussion of such diverse themes as the dreams described in Jensen's *Gradiva* (1907, p. 76), the mechanism operating in hysterical attacks (1909a, pp. 229-230), the formation of a phobia (1909b, p. 83), and the dis-

[ 89 ]

placement of affects in obsessional neurosis (1909c, pp. 196-198).

We find the same omission of economic explanations in a later discussion of the dream work and symptom formation, which is remarkable in that it "places"[9] the mechanisms characteristic of the primary process *between* two systems, indicating that the primary process is not restricted to one system, or, in structural terms, to the id (see p. 101).

> . . . the 'dream-work' . . . deserves our closest theoretical interest, since we are able to study in it, as nowhere else, what unsuspected psychical processes can occur in the unconscious, or rather, to put it more accurately, *between* two separate psychical systems like the conscious and unconscious. Among these freshly discovered psychical processes those of *condensation* and *displacement* are especially noticeable. The dream-work is a special case of the effects produced by two different mental groupings on each other —that is, of the consequences of mental splitting; and it seems identical in all essentials with the process of distortion which transforms the repressed complexes into symptoms where there is unsuccessful repression [1910, p. 36].

When Freud contrasted the "decomposition" of object representations in the paranoid delusion with the process of condensation in hysterical symptom formation, he likewise did not speak in terms of the economic point of view.

> . . . there is another feature in the development of Schreber's delusions which claims our attention. If we take a survey of the delusions as a whole, we see that the persecutor is divided into Flechsig and God. . . . In the later stages of the illness the decomposition of Flechsig goes further still. . . . A process of decomposition of this kind is very characteristic of paranoia. Paranoia decomposes just as hysteria condenses. Or rather, paranoia resolves once more into their elements

9 In Freud's topographical ("systemic") framework.

the products of the condensations and identifications which are effected in the unconscious [1911a, p. 49].

We can see from the following quotations that Freud's statements concerning the mechanisms of the primary process were meant first of all to reveal the working of certain unconscious thought processes to our understanding, and that the economic formulations were attempts at furnishing one such explanatory concept:

The dream-work is a psychological process the like of which has hitherto been unknown to psychology. It has claims upon our interest in two main directions. In the first place, it brings to our notice novel processes such as 'condensation' (of ideas) and 'displacement' (of psychical emphasis from one idea to another), processes which we have never come across at all in our waking life, or only as the basis of what are known as 'errors in thought'. In the second place, it enables us to detect the operation in the mind of a play of forces which was concealed from our conscious perception. We find that there is a 'censorship', a testing agency, at work in us, which decides whether an idea cropping up in the mind shall be allowed to reach consciousness, and which, so far as lies within its power, ruthlessly excludes anything that might produce or revive unpleasure. And it will be recalled at this point that in our analysis of parapraxes we found traces of this same intention to avoid unpleasure in remembering things and of similar conflicts between mental impulses.

A study of the dream-work forces on us irresistibly a view of mental life which appears to decide the most controversial problems of psychology. The dream-work compels us to assume the existence of an *unconscious* psychical activity which is more comprehensive and more important than the familiar activity that is linked with consciousness. . . . It enables us to dissect the psychical apparatus into a number of different agencies or systems, and shows us that in the system of unconscious mental activity processes operate which are of quite another kind from those perceived in consciousness [1913b, pp. 170-171].

In his papers on metapsychology, especially "The Unconscious" (1915c) and "A Metapsychological Supplement to the Theory of Dreams" (1917a), Freud's emphasis in discussing the primary process shifted to explanatory formulations utilizing the economic point of view. In fact, it was in "The Unconscious" that Freud coined the term "economic point of view" (p. 181).[10] Freud even arrived at what seemed like an equation when he said:

> To sum up: *exemption from mutual contradiction, primary process* (mobility of cathexes), *timelessness,* and *replacement of external by psychical reality*—these are the characteristics which we may expect to find in processes belonging to the system *Ucs.* [1915c, p. 187].

However, even here it seems quite obvious that the economic formulation was not a description of observed phenomena but a hypothesis attempting to make the mysterious working of "The *Ucs.*" more accessible to our understanding. Freud outlined "the special characteristics of the system *Ucs.*" as follows:

The distinction we have made between the two psychical systems receives fresh significance when we observe that processes in the one system, the *Ucs.*, show characteristics which are not met with again in the system immediately above it.

The nucleus of the *Ucs.* consists of instinctual representatives which seek to discharge their cathexis; that is to say, it consists of wishful impulses. These instinctual impulses are co-ordinate with one another, exist side by side without being influenced by one another, and are exempt from mutual contradiction. When two wishful impulses whose aims must appear to us incompatible become simultaneously active, the two impulses do not diminish each other or cancel each other out, but combine to form an intermediate aim, a compromise.

10 See Chapter 3.

[ 92 ]

There are in this system no negation, no doubt, no degrees of certainty; all this is only introduced by the work of the censorship between the *Ucs.* and the *Pcs.* Negation is a substitute, at a higher level, for repression. In the *Ucs.* there are only contents, cathected with greater or lesser strength.

The cathectic intensities [in the *Ucs.*] are much more mobile. By the process of *displacement* one idea may surrender to another its whole quota of cathexis; by the process of *condensation* it may appropriate the whole cathexis of several other ideas. I have proposed to regard these two processes as distinguishing marks [*als Anzeichen*] of the so-called *primary psychical process* [1915c, p. 186].

The mechanisms of displacement and condensation, explained in economic terms as occurring through mobility of cathectic intensities, were to Freud only *indicators* (possibly a more precise translation of "*Anzeichen*" than "distinguishing marks") that the "so-called primary psychical process" was operating, the latter also encompassing all the other aspects described in the preceding paragraphs.

That Freud *required* economic formulations only in a special context can be seen from his discussion of the concept condensation in the *Introductory Lectures*. For example:

The first achievement of the dream-work is *condensation*. By that we understand the fact that the manifest dream has a smaller content than the latent one, and is thus an abbreviated translation of it. Condensation can on occasion be absent; as a rule it is present, and very often it is enormous. It is never changed into the reverse; that is to say, we never find that the manifest dream is greater in extent or content than the latent one. Condensation is brought about (1) by the total omission of certain latent elements, (2) by only a fragment of some complexes in the latent dream passing over into the manifest one and (3) by latent elements which have something in common being combined and fused into a single unity in the manifest dream [1916-1917, p. 171].

Freud might have added an economic formulation here as a hypothesis of how the "mental apparatus" was able to perform this task.

We can easily see from most of Freud's dream examples that he used the term condensation in the context of "thought processes."

> *His father was dead but had been exhumed and looked bad. He had been living since then and the dreamer was doing all he could to prevent him noticing it. . . .*
> His father was dead; we know that. His having been exhumed did not correspond to reality; and there was no question of reality in anything that followed. But the dreamer reported that after he had come away from his father's funeral, one of his teeth began to ache. He wanted to treat the tooth according to the precept of Jewish doctrine: 'If they tooth offend thee, pluck it out!' And he went off to the dentist. But the dentist said: 'One doesn't pluck out a tooth. One must have patience with it. I'll put something into it to kill it; come back in three days and I'll take it out.'
> 'That "take out",' said the dreamer suddenly, 'that's the exhuming!'
> Was the dreamer right about this? It only fits more or less, not completely; for the *tooth* was not taken out, but only something in it that had died. But inaccuracies of this kind can, on the evidence of other experiences, well be attributed to the dream-work. If so, the dreamer had condensed his dead father and the tooth that had been killed but retained; he had fused them into a unity. No wonder, then, that something senseless emerged in the manifest dream, for, after all, not everything that was said about the tooth could fit his father. Where could there possibly be a *tertium comparationis* . . . between the tooth and his father, to make the condensation possible?
> But no doubt he must have been right, for he went on to say that he knew that if one dreams of a tooth falling out it means that one is going to lose a member of one's family [1916-1917, p. 188].

This applied also to his use of these concepts in explaining symptom formation:

> We must . . . remember that the same processes belonging to the unconscious play a part in the formation of symptoms as in the formation of dreams— namely, condensation and displacement. A symptom, like a dream, represents something as fulfilled: a satisfaction in the infantile manner. But by means of extreme condensation that satisfaction can be compressed into a single sensation or innervation, and by means of extreme displacement it can be restricted to one small detail of the entire libidinal complex [1916-1917, p. 366].

Or:

> Let us take as an example a case of hysterical headache or lumbar pain. Analysis shows us that, by condensation and displacement, it has become a substitutive satisfaction for a whole number of libidinal phantasies or memories [1916-1917, pp. 390-391].

He made an identical use of the concept of displacement (and also of transforming into the opposite), without resorting to economic formulations, in his classic analysis of the "wolf dream."

> *The fear of being eaten up by the wolves.* It seemed to the dreamer as though the motive force of this fear was not derived from the content of the dream. He said he need not have been afraid, for the wolves looked more like foxes or dogs, and they did not rush at him as though to bite him, but were very still and not at all terrible. We observe that the dream-work tries for some time to make the distressing content harmless by transforming it into its opposite. ('They aren't moving, and, only look, they have the loveliest tails!') Until at last this expedient fails, and the fear breaks out. It expresses itself by the help of the fairy tale, in which the goat-children are eaten up by the wolf-father. This part of

[ 95 ]

the fairy tale may perhaps have acted as a reminder of threats made by the child's father in fun when he was playing with him; so that the fear of being eaten up by the wolf may be a reminiscence as well as a substitute by displacement [1918, p. 44].

In *Beyond the Pleasure Principle* (1920) the concept primary process was first introduced in genetic terms in the context of a discussion of the replacement of the pleasure principle by the reality principle (p. 10). Later, however, Freud used economic formulations extensively. Although he discussed such terms as psychic energy, discharge, and cathexis as psychological concepts, nowhere is the link to neurophysiological formulations as close as in the following paragraph of this work:

It will perhaps not be thought too rash to suppose that the impulses arising from the instincts do not belong to the type of *bound nervous processes* [the last two words italicized by me], but of *freely mobile* processes which press towards discharge. The best part of what we know of these processes is derived from our study of the dream-work. We there discovered that the processes in the unconscious systems were fundamentally different from those in the preconscious (or conscious) systems. In the unconscious, cathexes can easily be completely transferred, displaced and condensed. . . . I described the type of process found in the unconscious as the 'primary' psychical process, in contradistinction to the 'secondary' process which is the one obtaining in our normal waking life. Since all instinctual impulses have the unconscious systems as their point of impact, it is hardly an innovation to say that they obey the primary process. Again, it is easy to identify the primary psychical process with Breuer's freely mobile cathexis and the secondary process with changes in his bound or tonic cathexis. If so, it would be the task of the higher strata of the mental apparatus to bind the instinctual excitation reaching the primary process [1920, pp. 34-35].

[ 96 ]

This holds true even more for the Breuer discussion referred to by Freud. While Breuer claimed in the introductory part of his theoretical contribution to the *Studies on Hysteria* (1893-1895) that "Psychical processes will be dealt with in the language of psychology" (p. 185), his discussion of "Intracerebral Tonic Excitations" (pp. 192-202) resorted to neurophysiological assumptions, albeit hypothetical ones.

The last sentence of the passage from *Beyond the Pleasure Principle* quoted above is also remarkable in that Freud, when speaking about instinctual excitation reaching the primary process, was perhaps inadvertently equating the primary process with the "primary system."

Another use of the term "primary process" in *Beyond the Pleasure Principle* is to be found in the following statement:

> We have found that one of the earliest and most important functions of the mental apparatus is to bind the instinctual impulses which impinge on it, to replace the primary process prevailing in them by the secondary process *and* [my italics] convert their freely mobile cathectic energy into a mainly quiescent (tonic) cathexis. . . . [This] transformation occurs on *behalf* of the pleasure principle; the binding is a preparatory act which introduces and assures the dominance of the pleasure principle [p. 62].

This is important for two reasons: (1) the "conversion" of the "freely mobile cathexis of the primary process" is only one aspect of the transition from primary to secondary process; (2) the economic formulation was indispensable for Freud in discussing the functioning of the mental apparatus in terms of the pleasure-unpleasure principles (see Chapters 11 and 12).

We can also see that Freud used economic formulations of the primary process as explanatory hypotheses of the shift of libidinal and aggressive cathexes from one object to another, and of similar shifts in the transference situation (1923, p. 45).

[ 97 ]

No economic formulation was needed in a different context such as the following, when Freud said:

> On the basis of a number of experiences I am inclined to draw the conclusion that thought-transference of this kind comes about particularly easily at the moment at which an idea emerges from the unconscious, or, in theoretical terms, as it passes over from the 'primary process' to the 'secondary process' [1925c, p. 138].

Here Freud used the concepts primary and secondary processes for the "passing" of an idea (*Vorstellung*) from one process to the other, and again spoke of these two processes as functional units.

It is clear from the following quotations that Freud always saw in the primary process the summation of all the mental processes operating in the "deeper, unconscious layers of the mind."

> I have given the name of *dream-work* to the process which, with the co-operation of the censorship, converts the latent thoughts into the manifest content of the dream. It consists of a peculiar way of treating the preconscious material of thought, so that its component parts become *condensed,* its psychical emphasis becomes *displaced,* and the whole of it is translated into visual images or *dramatized,* and completed by a deceptive *secondary revision.* The dream-work is an excellent example of the processes occurring in the deeper, unconscious layers of the mind, which differ considerably from the familiar normal processes of thought. It also displays a number of archaic characteristics, such as the use of a *symbolism* (in this case of a predominantly sexual kind) which it has since also been possible to discover in other spheres of mental activity [1925b, p. 45].

That a specific state of psychic energy was a hypothetical concept for Freud is again evident from a passage in the *New Introductory Lectures* (1933) where Freud offered perhaps the most detailed description of the characteristics of the id.

[ 98 ]

It . . . seems that the energy of these instinctual impulses [in the id] is in a state different from that in the other regions of the mind, far more mobile and capable of discharge; otherwise the displacements and condensations would not occur which are characteristic of the id [1933, pp. 74-75].

The most pertinent of Freud's formulations for my interpretation of the concept primary process are from his last work, *An Outline of Psycho-Analysis* (1940):

The sole prevailing quality in the id is that of being unconscious. Id and unconscious are as intimately linked as ego and preconscious: indeed, in the former case the connection is even more exclusive. If we look back at the developmental history of an individual and of his psychical apparatus, we shall be able to perceive an important distinction in the id. Originally, to be sure, everything was id; the ego was developed out of the id by the continual influence of the external world. In the course of this slow development certain of the contents of the id were transformed into the preconscious state and so taken into the ego; others of its contents remained in the id unchanged, as its scarcely accessible nucleus. During this development, however, the young and feeble ego put back into the unconscious state some of the material it had already taken in, dropped it, and behaved in the same way to some fresh impressions which it *might* have taken in, so that these, having been rejected, could leave a trace only in the id. In consideration of its origin we speak of this latter portion of the id as the *repressed*. It is of little importance that we are not always able to draw a sharp line between these two categories of contents in the id. They coincide approximately with the distinction between what was innately present originally and what was acquired in the course of the ego's development. . . .

What . . . is the true nature of the state which is revealed in the id by the quality of being unconscious and in the ego by that of being preconscious and in what does the difference between them consist?

But of that we know nothing. And the profound obscurity of the background of our ignorance is scarcely illuminated by a few glimmers of insight. Here we have approached the still shrouded secret of the nature of the psychical. We assume, as other natural sciences have led us to expect, that in mental life some kind of energy is at work; but we have nothing to go upon which will enable us to come nearer to a knowledge of it by analogies with other forms of energy. We seem to recognize that nervous or psychical energy occurs in two forms, one freely mobile and another, by comparison, bound; we speak of cathexes and hypercathexes of psychical material, and even venture to suppose that a hypercathexis brings about a kind of synthesis of different processes—a synthesis in the course of which free energy is transformed into bound energy. Further than this we have not advanced. . . .

Behind all these uncertainties, however, there lies one new fact, whose discovery we owe to psycho-analytic research. We have found that processes in the unconscious or in the id obey different laws from those in the preconscious ego. We name these laws *in their totality* [my italics] the *primary process,* in contrast to the *secondary process* which governs the course of events in the preconscious, in the ego [1940, pp. 163-164].

These "laws" prevail in the unconscious or in the id, as follows:

From the evidence of the existence of these two tendencies to condensation and displacement our theory infers that in the unconscious id the energy is in a freely mobile state and that the id sets more store by the possibility of discharging quantities of excitation than by any other consideration; and our theory makes use of these two peculiarities in defining the character of the primary process we have attributed to the id.

. . . The governing rules of logic carry no weight in the unconscious; it might be called the Realm of the Illogical. Urges with contrary aims exist side by side in the unconscious without any need arising for an adjustment between them. Either they have no influence whatever on each other, or, if they have, no decision is reached, but a compromise comes about which is nonsensical since it embraces mutually incompatible details [pp. 168-169].

Or:

The processes which are possible in and between the assumed psychical elements in the id (the *primary process*) differ widely from those which are familiar to us through conscious perception in our intellectual and emotional life; nor are they subject to the critical restrictions of logic, which repudiates some of these processes as invalid and seeks to undo them [p. 198].

When Freud said specifically that "We name these laws *in their totality* the primary process," it became obvious that his energy-economic formulations pertaining to the primary process represented only an attempt to illuminate our areas of ignorance by a "few glimmers of insight."

I have tried to document my contention that the economic formulation was seen by Freud only as an explanatory aspect of the broader concept primary process, by tracing the use of this concept and of such principal mechanisms as condensation and displacement in Freud's work from 1900 to 1939.

In view of the fact that Freud—without changing his basic formulation—used the term primary process either in its broader meaning or its narrower, economic one (the latter whenever such a hypothetical construct was appropriate to the topic he was discussing), it is not surprising that this term has had various interpretations in the psychoanalytic literature.

The terms "primary-" or "secondary-process thinking" were frequently used in theoretical papers and even more often in clinical ones. "Primary-process thinking" was applied in genetic terms to infantile mental processes, implying such characteristics as condensation, displacement, heedlessness of the limits of logic, time, and space, the use of symbolism, etc. All these characteristics were attributed mainly, and often exclusively, to the id. This application of the term primary process, although not spelled out as such, was in line with the broader framework for Freud's use of this term which I described earlier. The term "secondary-process thinking" was used to describe thought processes which more or less followed the laws of logic, as was characteristic of the mental processes of the structure ego.

Such use of these terms did not exclude economic formulations: e.g., the kind of energy, the cathectic distribution characteristic of each of the two processes. Specifically, the id was conceived as operating with free, mobile, uninhibited, "unbound" nonneutralized energy; the ego with inhibited, "bound" energy showing various degrees of neutralization (Hartmann, 1950, 1952; Gill, 1963).

We must of course distinguish between the *use* of a concept in such contexts as clinical presentations and attempts to *define* it. I would point out only that such definitions, if they claim to be based on Freud's work, should distinguish between his broader formulations and his hypothetical use of the economic point of view. For obvious reasons I cannot review here all of the psychoanalytic literature on this topic; instead I shall select quotations which illustrate the foregoing discussion. Some authors use the term primary process alternately in its broader context and its economic (energy) one; some only in its broader meaning; some strongly rule out all formulations except those expressed in economic terms, while others include the economic construct along with the broader formulation.

Anna Freud, for one, uses the term primary process mainly in its broader sense, as can be seen from the following:

In the id the so-called 'primary process' prevails; there is no synthesis of ideas, affects are liable to displacement,

[ 102 ]

opposites are not mutually exclusive and may even coincide and condensation occurs as a matter of course. The sovereign principle which governs the psychic processes is that of obtaining pleasure [1936, p. 7].

In her most recent book (1965) she uses the term in an even wider sense; e.g.,

. . . advance from primary process to secondary process functioning, i.e., to be able to interpolate thought, reasoning, and anticipation of the future between wish and action directed toward fulfillment . . . [p. 92].

[Or when she speaks of] characteristics of primary process functioning such as generalizations, displacements, repetitiveness, distortions, exaggerations [p. 100].

In another framework she equates primary process with the dominance of the pleasure principle (p. 115). Nor does she hesitate to speak of "primary-process thinking."

Hartmann, in "Rational and Irrational Action" (1947), speaks of the regressive elements of our thoughts which are manifested in the tendency toward "agglutination" and "irradiation of values" (p. 47). He then says:

Both tendencies . . . influence our psychological thinking, they are frequently found at the base of errors in judgment in political thought, and generally wherever highly invested value judgments come into play. Their character of shifting accents, of establishing and severing connections of facts with disregard of the object structure makes us think of the *primary process* [p. 48].

In his discussion of the genetic aspect of defense mechanisms Hartmann states:

There are many points concerning the origin of defense mechanisms that we have not yet come to understand. . . . It seems reasonable to assume that these mechanisms do

[ 103 ]

not originate as defenses in the sense we use the term once the ego as a definable system has evolved. . . . They may originate in other areas, and in some cases these primitive processes may have served different functions, before they are secondarily used for what we specifically call defense in analysis. The problem is to trace the genetic connections between those primordial functions and the defense mechanisms of the ego. Some of these may be modeled after some form of instinctual behavior. . . . We will also think of how the ego can use, for defense, characteristics of the primary process, as in displacement (Anna Freud, 1936) [1950, p. 124].

He makes similar use of the concept primary process in later publications:

A further complication is added by the fact that we know a rather wide field of phenomena that we could describe as Janus-faced in the sense that one aspect shows the primary and the other the secondary process. To use Anna Freud's (1936) example, in displacement as a mechanism of defense, a characteristic of the primary process is used for the purposes of the ego. This we also clearly see in dreams [1952, p. 172].

One aspect of language plays an essential part in Freud's psychology of schizophrenia. It is the fact that words are subject to the primary process; or that they are treated as if they were things [1953, p. 188].

Direct observation of psychotic patients confirmed on a large scale what Freud had inferred about the *characteristics and main contents* of primary processes [1958, p. 315; my italics].

These are examples of the use of primary process in what I have called the broader framework of Freud's formulation. That for Hartmann the economic formulation is also an attempt—perhaps the most important one—to explain mental functioning, can be seen from the following statement:

> *To account for the difference* in the unconscious and the conscious (and preconscious) processes Freud postulated two forms of energy distribution, conceptualized as, respectively, primary and secondary processes. The primary processes represent a tendency to immediate discharge, while the secondary processes are guided by the consideration of reality. This distinction is again both theoretically significant and clinically quite helpful. The thesis that behavior is to be explained also in terms of its energic cathexis is what we call, in analysis, the economic viewpoint [1959, p. 327; my italics].

Whenever Hartmann uses the term primary process in the context of his concept of neutralization, which has proved to be so fruitful for our understanding of the development and functioning of the structures ego and superego, his emphasis is on the economic formulation.

We can discern an equally varied use of the term primary process in the work of Ernst Kris. When he uses this term for the interpretation of "psychotic art," he is referring to its broader meaning, as a few examples will illustrate:

> We are familiar with the primary process mainly from the part it plays in dreams, in which the residue of infantile, preverbal thought processes survives. But the work of the primary process is not confined to dreams; it can be found in numerous pathological conditions and in many phenomena on the border of normalcy. Their common characteristic seems to be that the ego suffers a temporary or permanent loss of some of its functions. . . . The various mechanisms of the primary process do not contribute in an equal measure to the phenomena to be described in what follows. We shall find relatively little use of displacement. . . . On the other hand, we shall frequently encounter

condensation and the use of symbols in manifold variations [1936, pp. 98-99].

The representational creations of psychotics, being attempts at restitution, follow the laws of the primary process, the "language" of the id [p. 116].

[In his discussion of laughter Kris says:] The pleasure gain from regression shows us that the adult requires a certain cathexis, i.e., expenditure of energy, to curb in himself the working methods of the primary process, which breaks through in the infantile modes of thought contained in the comic of adults [1939, p. 221].

The broader interpretation of primary process is unequivocally intended in the following passage:

It is the other component, however—the well of inspiration or so-called "primary process"—that is of the most immediate interest. For it is in this aspect of aesthetic creation that ambiguity is most prominent. The symbols functioning in the primary process are . . . "overdetermined" . . . Such overdetermination is characteristic of almost all purposive action; but it is especially marked when the psychic level from which the behavior derives is close to the primary process. Words, images, fancies come to mind because they are emotionally charged; and the primary process exhibits to a striking degree the tendency to focus in a single symbol a multiplicity of references and thereby fulfill at once a number of emotional needs [Kris and Kaplan, 1948, p. 254].

The emphasis shifts to economic formulations, however, when Kris discusses the relationship between sublimation and neutralization. There he says:

Freud's distinction between primary and secondary processes was based on the idea that in the former energy was fluid, ready for immediate discharge, in the latter, bound, at the disposal of the ego [1952a, p. 27].

[ 106 ]

Economic formulations prevail in the joint papers of Hartmann, Kris, and Loewenstein. For example:

Functions of the id are characterized by the great mobility of cathexes of the instinctual tendencies and their mental representatives, i.e., by the operation of the primary process. Its manifestations are condensation, displacement, and the use of special symbols [1946, p. 31].

In the first sentence mobility of cathexes and primary process are more or less equated. The second sentence, however, makes a crucial point, namely, that mobility of cathexes is a hypothetical construct, while the manifestations of condensation and displacement and the use of special symbols are empirical phenomena (see also Gill, 1963, p. 109).

In another context Hartmann, Kris, and Loewenstein enumerate some of the explanatory assumptions concerning mental functioning as follows:

Psychoanalytic assumptions on psychic structure and the interrelation of its parts, on the function of psychic energy and its working, on the distinction of degrees of neutralization, of mobile and bound energies, and hence of primary and secondary processes, supply the best, or more precisely, the only set of assumptions which at present permits an explanatory approach to mental functioning [1951, p. 94].

This statement is in a sense an elaboration of Freud's formulation in the *Outline* (see above). However, while Freud specifically subsumed under the term primary process the laws regulating the mental processes in the id *"in their totality,"* Hartmann, Kris, and Loewenstein in this context (in contrast to the previously quoted passages from Hartmann and Kris) equate the term primary process with its economic formulation.

[ 107 ]

Schilder (1930) summarized most of the mechanisms of the primary process as:

(1) Distinction between internal and external reality is absent. (2) Experiences are timeless. (3) Displacements, condensations, and symbolizations take place. (4) The law of contradiction is suspended. (5) The cathexes are mobile and affect-quantities can be transferred completely from one idea to another [quoted by Rapaport, 1951b, p. 577, n. 297].

This last hypothesis, I have contended, is a construct designed to explain the working of such mechanisms as displacement and condensation.

The concept primary process was one of the main topics under discussion at a panel on "The Psychoanalytic Theory of Thinking" (see Arlow, 1958), in the course of which Fisher suggested that the term primary process be used in its broader meaning and not be restricted to its economic formulation. Fisher indicated that what was in *The Interpretation of Dreams* a very broad concept of the primary process, one which was equated with the dream work and all its mechanisms, was transformed in the paper on "The Unconscious" and in the structural hypothesis into a much narrower concept. The narrower concept retained the restricted meaning of the high mobility of cathexis utilizing condensation and displacement (see Arlow, 1958, p. 146).[11]

Arlow noted that the structural hypothesis was introduced into psychoanalysis for good cause. The earlier model of the psychic apparatus, based primarily on the economy of drive discharge and formalized in Chapter VII of *The Interpretation of Dreams,* had not held up in many respects. Our views on the subject of thinking must be brought in line with the wider revision of our frame of reference and

[11] I have quoted many passages which indicate that Freud used the broader concept not only after the publication of "The Unconscious" (1915c), but also after his introduction of the structural point of view (1923).

[ 108 ]

we cannot at the same time use conflicting concepts derived from an earlier, more limited set of hypotheses.

It would be incorrect, he said, to equate id, *the* Ucs and the primary process in spite of the fact that they have certain characteristics in common.[12] Accordingly, Arlow maintained, the term primary process should be reserved for the phenomenon of mobility of discharge of drive cathexis manifest pre-eminently through the mechanisms of displacement and condensation [pp. 148-149].

. . . many of the data of developmental psychology could be formulated much more effectively with a hypothesis utilizing primary process *tendencies* [my italics] to achieve, in the face of frustration, a perception identical with the memory traces of earlier gratification [p. 150].

In line with Arlow's discussion, Arlow and Brenner, in their recent monograph (1964), emphatically state their opinion that the term primary process should be restricted to its economic formulation, any other usage being deemed "inadmissible."[13]

12 No one (certainly not Fisher) tries to "equate" the id, the *Ucs.*, and the primary process. No one doubts that there is a basic difference between *pars pro toto* and *totum*. The primary process has always been described as one of the main characteristics of the id, but not identical with it. It has always been maintained that instinctual drives use, or "try" to use, primary-process mechanisms for discharge. This assumption does not imply that instinctual drives and primary process are equatable.

13 An example of different statements about the primary process used by the same authors (at an earlier time) is the following from Brenner's *Elementary Textbook of Psychoanalysis* (1955, p. 56): "Each of the terms 'primary process' and 'secondary process' is used in the psychoanalytic literature to refer to two related but distinct phenomena. The words, 'primary process,' for example, may refer either to a certain type of thinking which is characteristic for the child whose ego is still immature, or to the way in which we believe drive energy, whether libidinal or aggressive, is shifted about, and discharged in the id or in the immature ego. In an analogous way, 'secondary process' may refer to a type of thinking which is characteristic for the mature ego or it may refer to the processes of binding and mobilization of psychic energy which are believed to occur in the mature ego. The two types of thinking have the greater clinical importance and are fairly accessible to study. The two ways of dealing with and discharging psychic energy occupy a more important place in our theory, but are less accessible to study, as is true for all our hypotheses concerning psychic energy."

As we shall see later, this tendency to reduce primary process to an energy concept was eventually paralleled by a tendency to reduce the id as well to an energy (economic) concept. There is something paradoxical in the line of reasoning Arlow lays down in his panel discussion. On the one hand, he finds Freud's earlier model of the mental apparatus invalid—outmoded—because it was based primarily on the economy of drive discharge; on the other hand, he insists in the very next paragraph that the term primary process be reserved for the phenomenon of mobility of discharge of drive cathexis, thus using the same economic formulation that Freud had used as a hypothetical construct of the operation of what he was then (1900) still calling the primary and secondary $\psi$-systems. Yet the implication of Arlow's statement is what I have been pointing out in the foregoing discussion: we must distinguish between the functional manifestations of a structure or process and hypothetical constructs which attempt to account for some of these manifestations.

It is perhaps equally paradoxical that after insisting on reserving the term primary process for the phenomenon of discharge of drive cathexis, Arlow (1958) speaks of "primary process tendencies to achieve . . . a perception identical with memory traces of earlier gratification."

We must apply the same approach to the concept primary process that Hartmann (1939, 1964) and Hartmann, Kris, and Loewenstein (1946) have utilized for their formulations on psychic structure; that is to say, they define the psychic systems and their three substructures in terms of functions which show certain characteristics. Economic concepts such as neutralization (desexualization) of instinctual energy can be used on the one hand as an explanatory hypothesis about specific manifestations of function (e.g., sublimation, desomatization, etc.), while on the other hand the degree of neutralization, or its failure, can be deduced from certain characteristics of ego functioning ranging from the high degree of neutralization in problem solving (Kris, 1952b) to the breakdown of neutralization in certain schizophrenic manifestations (Hartmann, 1953) or in the resomatization of responses in "psychosomatic" illness (Schur, 1955). In short: metapsychological formulations should not be restricted to supporting any one of the metapsychological points of view. It is one of the "beauties" of the metapsychological points of view that they complement each other so meaningfully.

Even in the light of my contention that Freud saw the primary process as a broader concept than one based on a strictly economic point of view, the term "primary-process thinking" does not conform with Freud's terminology. For various reasons, Freud drew a distinction in his papers on metapsychology (1915b, 1915c, 1917a) between such terms as impulse, idea, and thought.

1. This distinction was in line with the formulations in *The Interpretation of Dreams* concerning the "circuitous path" which the secondary system has to choose to establish perceptual identity.

2. It also conformed to later formulations about the difference between imagery, fantasies based on perceptual identity, and thoughts based on word identity.

3. It was in line with Freud's continuing attempts to delineate first the "systems" and later the "structures" of the mental apparatus.[14]

4. The strict delineation between "impulses" and "thoughts" was also necessary as long as Freud's affect theory was formulated chiefly in terms of the dynamic and economic points of view (Rapaport, 1953).

5. Freud needed economic formulations to explain the countercathectic operations in repression (see Chapter 3).

14 It had been essential for Freud, in the prestructural era especially, to formulate such delineations mainly in terms of the economic point of view.

[ 111 ]

And yet when we bear in mind Freud's constant recommendation to think of all psychic processes in terms of a continuum;[15] when we remember that he spoke of the ego as merging with the id, an opinion he also expressed in his diagrams of the mental apparatus (1923, 1933)—then the strict distinction between impulses, mental processes, ideas, and thoughts becomes artificial. To assert that "Urges with contrary aims exist side by side in the unconscious" (1940, p. 169), or to speak of "processes . . . in and between the . . . psychical elements in the id" which are not "subject to the critical restrictions of logic" (1940, p. 198) and to deny to these impulses, processes, mental elements, and ideas the status of thoughts would seem to disregard the basic concept of a continuum.

A formulation preferable to "primary-process thinking" is the one used by Rapaport: "thought organized according to the primary or secondary process" (1951b, p. 487). Gill (1963) simply uses the term "mental contents organized on the level of primary or secondary process," thereby avoiding a definite stand on whether such "contents" should be assigned the status of thoughts. As long as we think in terms of a continuum, it becomes a matter of semantics whether we speak of contents, ideas, or thoughts. Obviously the term "impulses" would lean more toward a formulation exclusively economic in point of view, while "thought processes organized according to the primary [or secondary] process" would lean more toward a formulation reflecting the structural, genetic, economic, and adaptive points of view.

In line with the consistent application of the concept of a continuum, it is self-evident that "thought processes organized according to the primary process" cannot be restricted to the structure id, but must also be used by the ego (see Kris, 1952b;

15 See also Hartmann (1950, 1952, 1953) on degrees of neutralization; and Kris (1952b) on various continua of "preconscious thought processes."

Hartmann, 1955; Rapaport, 1951b). I have consistently applied this assumption in my discussions of anxiety and phobias, the various stratifications of danger, and the responses to the latter (1953, 1955, 1958, 1962). I have also pointed out a correlation between the relative prevalence of thought processes organized either according to the primary or to the secondary process and the degree of neutralization attained. I have assumed that this correlation is also significant in the resomatization of various affect responses. The assumption that thought processes organized according to the primary process must also take place in the ego is implicit in every discussion of primitive wishes, fantasies, and defenses. This was specifically postulated by Fisher in his panel contribution (see Arlow, 1958). Gill has pointed out in great detail in his monograph that such an assumption can be deduced from various formulations of Freud's. Rapaport (1957, 1960b) emphasized the importance of assuming the existence of an undifferentiated phase if we are to understand the development of both the primary and secondary processes. He postulates that both must be understood in terms of innate givens (primary autonomous apparatuses) and their maturation and development in interaction with environmental (experiential) factors. He stresses that we can speak at various stages of development of various *degrees* of dominance of primary and secondary process. There is an evident parallel here with the development of the id, and more specifically with the genesis of the wish, which I discussed in Chapter 7. Arlow (1958), in his panel contribution, and Arlow and Brenner (1964) restrict their consideration of the fact that the ego can also operate on the level of the primary process to the strictly economic formulation of this concept.

*There is general agreement, however, that the mental processes operating in the id, whether we speak of these as involving "psychical elements"* (Freud, 1940, p. 198), *"aims"*

[ 113 ]

(Hartmann, 1952, p. 164), *"contents"* (Kris, 1950, p. 306; Gill, 1963) *or, as I would propose, the most primitive thought processes underlying the concept "wish," are exclusively organized according to the primary process.*[16]

The implication of the preceding discussion is simply this: that we must view the primary process, too, as a continuum. The mental functions organized according to the primary process range, therefore, from the most primitive elements that we attribute to the id, based chiefly on primitive perception and memory traces, to such relatively complex processes as fantasies (Beres, 1962), also based on the memory traces of object and word representations. This is in accordance with the now generally accepted assumption that we can detect elements of all three structures of the mental apparatus in most manifestations of mental life. (This applies, of course, to the phase in which the structures ego and superego—whatever their level of maturation—have already developed.)

The preceding discussion has indicated the tendency that has been shown by some authors to restrict the concept primary process exclusively to an energy (economic) formulation.

[16] After completing this manuscript I was permitted to read an unpublished paper by Holt (1962) as well as his comments (1962) on an unpublished manuscript by Fisher on the primary process. This material deserves a thorough discussion, but I can mention here only certain points which are especially pertinent to this discussion.

1. Holt enlarges upon the concept presented by Rapaport (1957-1959) who states that the primary process is organized upon the "drive organization of memories." Holt postulates "an association of all the experiences of the infant at the moment when the drive is active and satisfied" (see Chapter 8).

2. Holt also assumes that there is a development and a certain "structuralization" of the primary process.

3. He assumes, too, that Freud's formulations about the primary process included noneconomic explanations.

4. He assumes that the primary process is not restricted to the id.

5. It is therefore not surprising that Holt indicates in his private communication to Fisher that: (a) he does not restrict the concept primary process to its economic formulation despite the advantage of the latter's simplicity; (b) he does not subscribe to the idea that the id is completely unorganized but would suggest that we "build on statements of Freud's that attribute structure to it, rather than on those statements that portray it as chaos."

Support for such a tendency has been drawn from economic formulations made in connection with the structural concept in general and certain aspects of ego psychology in particular.

The next step was to reduce the id to an energy concept.

Such tendencies, and the objections to them, were considered extensively at the panel discussion on "The Concept of the Id" (see Marcovitz, 1963).

In this view the id would have no content, no structure.[17] It would be a "seething cauldron" of energies. A strict delineation would have to be made between energic impulses, ideas, wishes, mental representations, memory, perception, and fantasies. But this is not all. We could no longer say, for instance, that the ego "mediates between the demands of the id and the environment." We could speak about instinctual danger only in terms of quantities of energy. The whole concept "conflict" would have to be reformulated.

We could no longer speak of an *inter*systemic conflict between the ego and the id—unless we phrased it as a conflict between the ego and "an energy" or between various types of energy. The next step would be to speak of defenses and dangers only in economic terms. If we followed this line of thinking to its logical conclusion, we would have to end up not only with a purely economical model but with a "physiological" one as well.[18]

17 In recent papers Beres (1962, 1965) has on the one hand strongly insisted that the term "structure" be limited to the three structures of the mental apparatus: id, ego, and superego, and has objected to the use made of this term by Hartmann (1964), Rapaport (1960b), Gill (1963), and many others; on the other hand he has also objected to the assignment of any structuralization or content to the id.

18 The latter term is, of course, not meant to exclude the fact that what Freud called the "physical or somatic processes which are concomitant with the psychical ones" (1940, p. 157) have their physiological substrata. For the time being, we must operate with psychological concepts, with the understanding that they are constructs. Neurophysiology and information theory have gone a long way. However, as Fisher (1965) has stated, we can now conceptualize and explain physiologically the process of dreaming, but not the dream itself.

[ 115 ]

When Freud spoke of the "psychical elements in the id" he was obviously speaking of "contents."

It is interesting that the economic formulations, which were intended only as hypothetical explanations of certain *manifestations* of mental functioning, should now be accepted more readily than the assumptions about these "psychical elements" which we can *observe* in the results of such mechanisms as condensation and displacement whenever we examine a dream, uncover unconscious primitive wishes, or detect what Hartmann calls "id aims."

Can it be that the inherent resistance against the existence and mode of operation of unconscious mental processes expresses itself in this manner?[19]

Let us never forget Freud's most incisive formulation which he arrived at near the end of his creative life, and which applies to both "psychic" reality and reality "proper":

The hypothesis we have adopted of a psychical apparatus extended in space, expediently put together, developed by the exigencies of life, which gives rise to the phenomena of consciousness only at one particular point and under certain conditions—this hypothesis has put us in a position to establish psychology on foundations similar to those of any other science, such, for instance, as physics. In our science as in the others the problem is the same: behind the attributes (qualities) of the object under examination which are presented directly to our perception, we have to discover something else which is more independent of the particular receptive capacity of our sense organs and which approximates more closely to what may be supposed to be the real state of affairs. We have no hope of being able to reach the latter itself, since it is evident that everything new that we have inferred must nevertheless be translated back into the language of our perceptions, from which it is simply impossible for us to free ourselves. But herein lies the

19 As we can see in the letter by Freud quoted in Chapter 1, he himself was constantly aware of this resistance.

very nature and limitation of our science. It is as though we were to say in physics: 'If we could see clearly enough we should find that what appears to be a solid body is made up of particles of such and such a shape and size and occupying such and such relative positions.' In the meantime we try to increase the efficiency of our sense organs to the furthest possible extent by artificial aids; but it may be expected that all such efforts will fail to affect the ultimate outcome. Reality will always remain 'unknowable' [1940, p. 196].[20]

We can operate with such concepts as the structures id-ego-superego and the "qualities" unconscious, preconscious, primary and secondary process, only if we keep in mind, as Freud pointed out again and again, and I have reiterated, that these concepts are constructs; that *there are no strict delineations in our mental life;* that Freud's concept of a *continuum* is the only valid one to apply to all of the above. Hartmann, Kris, and Loewenstein emphasize this by saying:

These three psychic substructures or systems are conceived of not as independent parts of personality that invariably oppose each other, but as three centers of psychic functioning that can be characterized according to their developmental level, the amount of energy vested in them, and their demarcation and interdependence at a given time. Under specific conditions one of the centers may expand its area, and another or the two others may recede; more correctly, we should say that functions exercised by one of the systems may temporarily be more or less influenced by one of the others [1946, p. 30].

Gill's tightly reasoned monograph says rightly:

The id *could* be defined as a chaos of completely free, uninhibited, and uncontrolled energy. In such a view the id has no structure and is therefore a fiction. I am not, of course, suggesting that because a concept is a fiction it may not

20 See Marie Bonaparte's letter of January 4, 1938 to Freud, in which she discusses Kant's formulations about space and time (Schur, 1965a).

have scientific value, but only that it should be recognized as such and that this particular fiction should not be mistaken for a structural concept.

If the id were regarded as such a fiction, *the conception of the mental apparatus would be reduced to the ego* [1963, p. 144; my italics].

He then decides against such an alternative, and assigns to the id content and memory, using Glover's (1947) term "microstructures," which should also be understood in a genetic sense. Gill's reasoning in assigning content (structure) to the id is presented convincingly and is in every way complementary to my presentation.

The application of the genetic point of view and of the concept of a continuum has also led me to the assumption that the id is "structural" and has "content." Moreover, as we saw earlier (Chapter 8), my discussion postulates the maturation and development of the id, a development which was described by Freud after his exposition of the various phases of psychosexual development. According to the view of the mental apparatus as an open system, the id is "supplied" by (a) somatic (physiological) sources; and (b) percepts and memory traces (see also Fisher and Paul, 1959; Eissler, 1962); and, according to Freud, (c) *also* "contains the repressed."[21]

That the id, too, is subject to maturation and development is one of the first genetic formulations advanced by Freud (1900, 1905c) long before he articulated the structural point of view. This postulate is inherent in the concept of an undifferentiated phase, and has repeatedly been stressed by Hartmann (for example, in 1952), so that it requires no further discussion.

---

[21] As Gill has pointed out, many of Freud's formulations, including certain passages from the *Outline,* might seem to indicate that Freud assigned only "the repressed" to the system *Ucs.* and the id. However, many of Freud's statements in the *Outline* indicate clearly that "the core" of the *Ucs.* or the id is not equated with "the repressed" (see, for example, 1940, pp. 145, 163, 197).

# 10

## The Id and the Aggressive Instinctual Drive

IN THE PRECEDING chapters, the id and the development of
the concept "wish" were discussed mainly in terms of the
libidinal instinctual drive.

Any attempt to discuss the *development* of the aggressive
instinctual drive must remain much more speculative. I have
assumed that the id develops under the influence of growth
and maturation of somatic structures, and that it utilizes—
as the ego does—certain primary autonomous apparatuses;
that all through life the instinctual drives keep receiving
"supplies" from physiological sources. This assumption also
applies to the development of the aggressive instinctual drive.

Animal life on every level of organization is based on
destruction.[1] The virus invades a living cell; a bird feeds on
countless worms; man is a voracious destroyer. Destruction of
an object presupposes, as indicated in connection with libidinal development, an approach response.[2] We can detect in
the evolutional development of destructive approach behavior
a similar shift from dependency on external stimulation to
internalization. This evolutional development repeats itself
to a certain extent in infancy. Only after a certain primitive
level of internalization has taken place can we speak of an
aggressive instinctual drive as a psychological concept, in con-

---

1 It is a matter of semantics whether plant life should also be included here.
2 Only modern man can use machines for destruction.

trast to certain biophysiological responses.[3] The discharge of the destructive drive may be triggered by instinctual (libidinal) demands, with the hungry infant as a paradigm.

The destructive drive has more or less species-specific aims and objects. We may also assume that every animal has some inborn apparatuses which act as inhibitors of *unrestricted* discharge of the aggressive drive.[4] Such inhibitors are partly physiological, e.g., the mechanism which protects the animal from eating itself to death (Kaufman, 1960); partly they are based on certain percepts (IRMs) which are responded to with particular species-specific inhibitions. Such percepts and the responses to them have a high survival value in that they prevent animals from killing their own offspring, and in general prevent intraspecies killing (see Schur 1958, 1960a, 1961a). The elimination or even blunting of certain percepts also ends the inhibition.

In Chapter 6 I discussed the impact of internalization on the evolutional series. In man, species-specific innate behavior patterns ("instinctive" behavior) play a much smaller role, even, than in higher animals (Lorenz, 1937). We can only speculate, therefore, whether and to what extent innate inhibitory structures (thresholds) play a role in the inhibition of the discharge of the aggressive drive.[5]

We assume that these, like any other threshold mechanisms, utilize preformed primary autonomous apparatuses (Hartmann, 1939, 1950; Rapaport, 1960b; Gill, 1963). They have survival value in an evolutionary sense, serving adaptation

[3] Here again no time table can be given.

[4] For an extensive discussion of the aggressive instinctual drive in animals and men, with special emphasis on its evolutionary aspects, see Lorenz (1964).

[5] Freud's discussion of the close relationship between the superego and id expresses such an assumption, formulated in accordance with his adherence to the Lamarckian theory of evolution. For a discussion of Freud's neo-Lamarckian attitude see L. Ritvo (1965) and Schur and Ritvo (1966).

not only by preventing intraspecies killing, but also by providing man with the substrate from which, through interaction with the environment, ego and superego structures can be built. They may also represent the substrate from which the function of neutralization develops.

In such threshold mechanisms we can trace (not without great difficulty in conceptualization) the development from a mechanism which can only be described in physiological terms to others where psychological concepts can be applied. In structural terms, such thresholds would have to be "placed" on the "borderline" between the id and the other structures.[6]

I have discussed the fact that the memory trace of the perception of need gratification is the matrix of the development of a wish. It is difficult to conceptualize the mental representation of the early gratification of the aggressive drive because, as mentioned earlier, the latter's discharge is originally triggered by libidinal demands. From our clinical experience we have reason to assume that the aggressive drive is also subject to regulation by the unpleasure and pleasure principles. As Freud repeatedly pointed out, we hardly ever see manifestations of the aggressive drive in its pure state. Its discharge is mostly combined with a discharge of the libidinal drive. When (in accord with Gill) I ascribed "content" to the id, I found it easier to detect such content in libidinal id manifestations.

We can assume, however, that the "content" of aggressive wishes (using the term wish as previously discussed) gives a certain behavioral aspect to the manifestation of such id derivatives, which are also expressions of libidinous wishes (e.g., the infant's biting of the mother after the eruption of

6 The quotation marks around "placed" and "borderline" are intended to convey my uneasiness over the use of "concrete," "topographic" terms in this context (see Freud's diagrams, 1923, 1933).

teeth, etc.). We may likewise ascribe "content" to such drive vicissitudes as the turning of aggression against the self.[7]

The development of hate is itself the result of a complex development (object development), and only the drive aspect —which is again more "amorphous" (nonstructured)—can be ascribed to the id (see Arlow, 1963; Schur, 1961a).

[7] This concept, too, presents great difficulties of conceptualization. It has been widely used to describe certain phenomena of early infancy which look to the *observer* like aggression turned against the self; for example, head banging, hair pulling, certain phenomena of somatization, etc.—all this during a period before separation or distinction between self and object has taken place. While all these phenomena may be manifestations of the aggressive drive, we cannot speak of *turning* against the self before self and object, inside and outside, have clearly been differentiated. It might be preferable and more accurate to speak of *autoaggressive* phenomena in analogy with *autoerotic* activities such as thumb sucking.

*Part II*

# 11

# *The Regulatory Principles of Mental Functioning*

IN CHAPTER 3 I referred to Freud's statement that the id "obeys" the pleasure-unpleasure principle without restriction. Similar statements about the relationship between the mental processes that take place in the id can be found in most of Freud's discussions of the id (see Chapters 3 and 5). Such conceptualizations of the interrelationship between the id and the pleasure-unpleasure principle have been greatly complicated by Freud's introduction of the "repetition compulsion" as a *superordinated* principle of mental functioning operating *beyond* the pleasure principle as an expression of the death instinct.

For this reason, as pointed out in the Introduction, a meaningful discussion of the pleasure-unpleasure principle, which in turn is intimately related to the concept id, must concern itself with the other regulatory principles. In the following chapters I shall therefore transcend the limits of the concept id. Moreover, in addition to refining theoretical formulations, I shall offer conclusions applicable to problems of psychoanalytic technique, especially in the phase of "working through."

The obstacles to a reconsideration of our theoretical concepts are especially formidable in a discussion of Freud's use of the concept "unpleasure-pleasure principle." The reasons for this are the following:

1. Freud himself used this concept differently at different times (e.g., 1900, 1911b, 1915a, 1920, 1923, 1924a, 1926, 1940).

2. In contrast to some other concepts, there was no consistent development of this concept; old formulations which in part had been replaced by later ones would return in still later works.

3. Freud used this concept not only within the framework of psychology (metapsychology), but also within the framework of various hypotheses borrowed from other branches of science.

4. When Freud spoke about the pleasure-unpleasure principle within a metapsychological framework, he resorted primarily to economic formulations;[1] but he also used experiential ones in which pleasure and unpleasure indicated affects within the framework of structural concepts.

5. Freud tried to adapt the concept "pleasure-unpleasure principle" to his evolving theories of instinctual drives, theories which in turn were influenced by his varying formulations of the unpleasure-pleasure principle. This interplay is especially evident in the theory of the death instinct, the "Nirvana" principle, and the "repetition compulsion."

6. Freud combined his formulation of this concept with his phylogenetic and ontogenetic formulations of the development of the "mental apparatus."

7. Few analysts (in fact, they are actually in the minority) who use the concepts pleasure-unpleasure, pleasure-pain principle, spell out precisely which of Freud's formulations they are actually referring to. This is especially confusing in any consideration of the relationship between the regulating prin-

[1] Formulations which we now categorize as economic or structural were made by Freud (1895, 1900) long before he had actually conceptualized the various points of view of metapsychology.

ciples and the affects pleasure and unpleasure, and in any discussion of those modes of functioning which Freud tried to explain in *Beyond the Pleasure Principle* (1920).

8. The "wedding" of the pleasure-unpleasure principle and the concept of the repetition compulsion to the death-instinct theory on the one hand made any explanation of the correlation of the regulating principle with the affects pleasure and unpleasure even more difficult, and on the other hand shifted the balance from conceptualization based on empirical facts to the formulation of hypotheses for which empirical data then had to be adduced.

It is my contention that it would be easier to avoid certain pitfalls, and would perhaps add to the usefulness of the concept, if we re-examined the various trains of thought (models) indicated by Freud in his earlier works, for example, Chapter VII of *The Interpretation of Dreams* (1900) and "Instincts and Their Vicissitudes" (1915a), and then tried to correlate them with his later formulations (1920, 1923, 1924a).

This re-examination requires, first, that we distinguish between a pleasure and an unpleasure principle.[2] The assumption of such a distinction enlarges upon Hartmann's formulation, according to which the avoidance of unpleasure is a special aspect of the pleasure principle. Hartmann states:

> . . . in man the pleasure principle is not a very reliable guide to self-preservation. There are, though, exceptions to this rule; the avoidance of pain (*Schmerz*), e.g., retains its biological significance. . . . In those situations in which pleasure in one system (id) would induce unpleasure in another one (ego), the child learns to use the danger signal (a dose of unpleasure) to mobilize the pleasure principle and in this way to protect himself. . . . He will not only

2 A distinction between the pleasure and unpleasure principles has recently also been suggested by Eidelberg (1962). His discussion, however, is predominantly concerned with the experiential (affect) aspect of pleasure and unpleasure.

use this mechanism against danger from within but also against danger from without. The process is directly guided by the pleasure principle; it is really the pleasure principle that gives this move its power. What interests us in this connection is that *through a special device, an aspect of the pleasure principle itself (avoidance of unpleasure) is made to serve one of the most essential functions we make use of in our dealings with reality* [1956a, p. 250; my italics].

It is also my contention that both the unpleasure and the pleasure principles[3] have survival value[4] and therefore serve adaptation, quite apart from the role they play in the formation of the reality principle (Hartmann, 1939, 1948, 1953, 1956a).

---

3 I shall henceforth refrain from speaking of one principle.

4 I use the term "survival value" in its evolutionary meaning, in preference to the term "self preservation." Freud himself abandoned his concept of an "instinct" of self preservation. Even ardent proponents of the "instinct" concept, such as the ethologists (Lorenz, 1952; Tinbergen, 1951), reject the notion of an "instinct" of self preservation. For a discussion see also Loewenstein (1940); for an opposing view see the discussion of the "instinct of self preservation" by White (1963).

# 12

## *The Unpleasure Principle*

THE CONCEPTS pleasure and unpleasure principles, as previously indicated, were formulated by Freud in the context of such genetic hypotheses as the development of the mental apparatus, and more specifically in the context of the discussion of his concepts of wish, instinctual drives, and the primary and secondary processes. I shall try to show that Freud used two main models for both the development of the mental apparatus and his concepts unpleasure and pleasure principles. These models have phylogenetic and ontogenetic implications.

The first model appeared in many of Freud's formulations, starting as early as 1892, and was subsequently restated in various terms throughout his work.[1] It is generally assumed to follow Fechner's "principle of constancy." However, on closer inspection we see that some of Freud's formulations do not quite conform to this principle. Freud quoted the following passage from Fechner in *Beyond the Pleasure Principle* (1920):

> Fechner's statement is to be found contained in a small work, *Einige Ideen zur Schöpfungs- und Entwicklungsgeschichte der Organismen,* 1873 (Part XI, Supplement, 94), and reads as follows: 'In so far as conscious impulses always have some relation to pleasure or unpleasure, pleas-

[1] See Strachey's numerous Editor's footnotes; e.g., *Standard Edition*, V, p. 565; XIV, pp. 119, 121; XVIII, p. 9.

[ 129 ]

ure and unpleasure too can be regarded as having a psycho-physical relation to conditions of stability and instability. This provides a basis for a hypothesis into which I propose to enter in greater detail elsewhere. According to this hypothesis, every psycho-physical motion rising above the threshold of consciousness is attended by pleasure in proportion as, beyond a certain limit, it approximates to complete stability, and is attended by unpleasure in proportion as, beyond a certain limit, it deviates from complete stability; while between the two limits, which may be described as qualitative thresholds of pleasure and unpleasure, there is a certain margin of aesthetic indifference. . . .'[1]

[1] [Cf. 'Project', end of Section 8 of Part I.—'Aesthetic' is here used in the old sense of 'relating to sensation or perception'.] [pp. 8-9].

This formulation of Fechner's was actually concerned primarily with the *experiences* of pleasure and unpleasure, but Freud used it as the basis for a biopsychological regulating principle[2] going beyond the aspect of complete stability. A few quotations from various works of Freud will illustrate this point.[3]

There can be no doubt that that apparatus has only reached its present perfection after a long period of development. Let us attempt to carry it back to an earlier stage of its functioning capacity. Hypotheses, whose justifications must be looked for in other directions, tell us that at first the apparatus's efforts were directed towards keeping itself *so far as possible free from stimuli;* consequently its first struc-

[2] Even at this point we can see how essential it is for a proper understanding of these "principles" that we make a distinction between economic and experiential formulations.

[3] In the pages that follow, a certain amount of repetition in quoting salient passages from Freud's work is unavoidable because of the overlapping content of his formulations on phylogenesis, the development of the id, and the pleasure-unpleasure principles. To avoid the confusion of referring the reader back to passages cited earlier in a different context, it seems advisable simply to repeat some of the quotations.

ture followed the plan of a reflex apparatus, so that any sensory excitation impinging on it could be promptly discharged along a motor path [1900, p. 565; my italics].

In "Instincts and Their Vicissitudes" (1915a) Freud expressed this thought as follows:

In order to guide us in dealing with the field of psychological phenomena, we do not merely apply certain conventions to our empirical material as basic *concepts;* we also make use of a number of complicated *postulates.* We have already alluded to the most important of these, and all we need now do is to state it expressly. This postulate is of a biological nature, and makes use of the concept of 'purpose' (or perhaps of expediency) and runs as follows: the nervous system is an apparatus which has the function of getting rid of the stimuli that reach it, or of reducing them to the lowest possible level; or which, *if it were feasible* [my italics], would maintain itself in an altogether unstimulated condition [pp. 119-120].

I return now to the paragraph in Chapter VII of *The Interpretation of Dreams* in which Freud first introduced his definition of "pleasure and unpleasure," without yet mentioning the concept of a regulatory principle:

We have already [p. 565 ff.] explored the *fiction* of a primitive psychical apparatus whose activities are regulated by an effort to avoid an accumulation of excitation and to *maintain itself so far as possible without excitation* [my italics]. For that reason it is built upon the plan of a reflex apparatus. The power of movement . . . is at its disposal as the path to discharge. We went on to discuss the psychical consequences of an 'experience of satisfaction'; and in that connection we were already able to add a second hypothesis . . .[4] that the accumulation of excitation . . . is felt as un-

[4] It is of interest that a fine point of Freud's formulation did not find its way into Strachey's translation of this passage (p. 598). The correct translation would read: "We *could have added* [or: *would have been able to add*] a second hypothesis" [my italics].

[ 131 ]

pleasure and that it sets the apparatus in action with a view to repeating the experience of satisfaction, which involved a diminution of excitation and was felt as pleasure [p. 598].[5]

In the paragraph in which Freud first introduced the term "unpleasure principle" (1900, Chapter VII)—the term "pleasure principle" was not introduced until later (1911b, p. 219) —a somewhat *different model* was used. I shall therefore turn first to other formulations in which Freud further elaborated on the equation of tension reduction with pleasure and an increase of tension with unpleasure. Such an elaboration introduced Freud's *Beyond the Pleasure Principle* (1920):

> In the theory of psycho-analysis we have no hesitation in assuming that the course taken by mental events is automatically regulated by the pleasure principle. We believe, that is to say, that the course of those events is invariably set in motion by an unpleasurable tension, and that it takes a direction such that its final outcome coincides with a lowering of that tension—that is, with an avoidance of unpleasure or a production of pleasure. In taking that course into account in our consideration of the mental processes which are the subject of our study, we are introducing an 'economic' . . . factor in addition to the 'topographical' and 'dynamic' ones, we shall, I think, be giving the most complete description of them of which we can at present conceive, and one which deserves to be distinguished by the term 'metapsychological' [p. 7].

In the very next paragraph Freud admitted that the concept "pleasure principle" was not meant to explain satisfactorily the "feelings of pleasure and unpleasure which act so imperatively upon us." One gets the impression that Freud introduced this cryptic discussion of the affective (experiential) aspect of pleasure and unpleasure only as a bridge to his quotation of Fechner's formulation, which takes as its point

5 See my discussion in Chapter 8.

of departure concepts of "stability" and "constancy." Freud
then quickly returned to the economic formulation when
he stated:

> The facts which have caused us to believe in the dom-
> inance of the pleasure principle in mental life also find
> expression in the hypothesis that the mental apparatus
> endeavours to keep the quantity of excitation present in it
> as low as possible or at least to keep it constant. This latter
> hypothesis is only another way of stating the pleasure prin-
> ciple; for if the work of the mental apparatus is directed
> towards keeping the quantity of excitation low, then any-
> thing that is calculated to increase that quantity is bound
> to be felt as adverse to the functioning of the apparatus,
> that is as unpleasurable. The pleasure principle follows
> from the principle of constancy: actually the latter prin-
> ciple was inferred from the facts which forced us to adopt
> the pleasure principle [p. 9].

To turn now to the model with which Freud introduced
his unpleasure principle (1900, Chapter VII):

> Let us examine the antithesis to the primary experience of
> satisfaction—namely, the experience of an external fright.
> Let us suppose that the primitive apparatus is impinged
> upon by a perceptual stimulus which is a source of painful
> excitation. Unco-ordinated motor manifestations will fol-
> low until one of them withdraws the apparatus from the
> perception and at the same time from the pain. If the per-
> ception re-appears, the movement will at once be repeated
> (a movement of flight, it may be) till the perception has
> disappeared once more. In this case, no inclination will
> remain to recathect the perception of the source of pain,
> either hallucinatorily or in any other way. On the contrary,
> there will be an inclination in the primitive apparatus to
> drop the distressing memory-picture immediately, if any-
> thing happens to revive it, for the very reason that if its
> excitation were to overflow into perception it would pro-
> voke unpleasure (or, more precisely, would *begin* to pro-

voke it). . . . [This] avoidance by the psychical process of the memory of anything that had once been distressing affords us the prototype . . . of *psychical repression.* . . .

As a result of the unpleasure principle, then, the first ψ-system is totally incapable of bringing anything disagreeable into the context of its thoughts [p. 600].

The model for this formulation is the response to an external, "painful," "frightening," or, to put it more generally, too *intense* stimulus. As already indicated (see Chapter 7), this model for a psychological mechanism has not only *biophysiological* but also *evolutionary* implications. It is evident that the model for Freud's unpleasure principle is the *necessity* for withdrawal[6]—physical withdrawal if the apparatuses for this are available,[7] withdrawal of the cathexis of the percept and later also of the memory trace of a "painful" excitation (Freud compared this mechanism to the ostrich policy [1900, p. 600]).

Clearly the withdrawal response, which on a biopsychological level is regulated by the unpleasure principle, has high survival value in evolutionary terms. For the phenotype both actual physical withdrawal and the withdrawal of cathexis from the perception and memory trace of painful stimulation re-establish equilibrium (stability, constancy).

We can now retrace the steps by which Freud arrived at his formulation of the unpleasure principle: he spoke of the model of a reflex apparatus which tries to maintain itself free of stimuli (1900, p. 598) and the activities of which are regulated by an effort to avoid an accumulation of tension, such an accumulation being equated with unpleasure; and finally, he arrived at the model of withdrawal from excessive

[6] That certain withdrawal responses, for instance, the blinking reflex, are the biological autonomous precursors of defenses has been stressed by Hartmann (1939, 1950, 1964).

[7] Such apparatuses are relatively poorly developed in the newborn (see Schur, 1962).

*external* stimulation, thus formulating the unpleasure principle.

The concern with excessive stimulation permeated Freud's theoretical and clinical formulations throughout the twenty years following his conceptualization of the unpleasure principle. In *Beyond the Pleasure Principle* (1920) Freud again took the response to intense, potentially traumatic external stimulation as the point of departure for far-reaching speculations.

> Let us picture a living organism in its most simplified possible form as an undifferentiated vesicle of a substance that is susceptible to stimulation. Then the surface turned towards the external world will from its very situation be differentiated and will serve as an organ for receiving stimuli. . . . This little fragment of living substance is suspended in the middle of an external world charged with the most powerful energies; and it would be killed by the stimulation emanating from these if it were not provided with a protective shield against stimuli. . . . *Protection against* stimuli is an almost more important function for the living organism than *reception of* stimuli [1920, pp. 26, 27].

It is obvious that the development of a "protective shield" (protective barrier, *Reizschutz*) is biologically as essential as the function of withdrawal. Both have eminent survival value and must have played an important role in evolution.[8]

Freud then carried his speculations further, formulating them partly in phylogenetic terms, and contending that in the course of evolution "the external cortical layer had mi-

---

[8] We know of the importance of the trauma concept in Freud's work. The discovery of the inherent character of infantile fantasies only changed Freud's formulations about the nature of the trauma, and not about its impact. Freud's *Moses and Monotheism* (1939), the last book published during his lifetime, contains a detailed discussion of the trauma concept. His discussion of trauma in *Beyond the Pleasure Principle* and its importance for the reformulation of his theory of instinctual drives and the pleasure-unpleasure principles will be discussed further in Chapter 15.

grated inwards." Ontogenetically, the central nervous system still develops out of the ectoderm.

The following two formulations made by Freud in this context are pertinent to my discussion:

(1) that there is a difference in the effectiveness of the protective barrier against stimulations arising from without as compared with those arising from within;

(2) that "a particular way is adopted of dealing with any internal excitations which produce too great an increase of unpleasure: there is a tendency to treat them as though they were acting, not from the inside, but from the outside, so that it may be possible to bring the shield against stimuli into operation as a means of defense against them. This is the origin of *projection,* which is destined to play such a large part in the causation of pathological processes" (1920, p. 29).

As mentioned earlier, however, genetically everything outside the "mental apparatus" is "external." The distinction between stimuli arising from within and from without the organism is a result of maturation and development.[9]

Freud's previously quoted definition of unpleasure as an "accumulation of excitation" is concerned with stimulation originating *within* the organism, but outside the "primitive apparatus." Freud stressed that "Most of the unpleasure that we experience is *perceptual* unpleasure" (1920, p. 11).

We may now state that while all the formulations and models presented thus far are influenced by the constancy principle, they all emphasize mainly the *necessity* of withdrawing from excessive stimulation in order to prevent tension, which is equated with unpleasure. All, in turn, are modeled after the automatic (reflex) withdrawal from excessive external stimulation, with reference to which Freud coined the term unpleasure principle. We may add that

9 Goethe said: "Whatever is inside, is outside."

Freud's "protective barrier" represents an additional safe-guard.

In summary: the unpleasure principle regulates the *necessity* to withdraw[10] from excessive stimulation impinging upon the mental apparatus from the outside, "outside" implying both outside the organism and outside the mental apparatus.

---

[10] Withdrawal is understood to include both the physical act of withdrawal and the withdrawal of special cathexes.

# 13

## *The Pleasure Principle*

No living organism can survive *only* by withdrawal from the excessive stimulation which causes unpleasure, or through protection by the stimulus barrier. Without approach responses no sustenance can be found. In lower animals most functioning, especially approach and withdrawal responses, is still overwhelmingly dependent on external stimulation; hence Descartes' statement: *"Animal non agit, agitur."*

I have already discussed (Chapter 7) the evolutional development of somatic apparatuses which have resulted in a gradual shift away from *primary* dependence on external stimulation. This evolutional development, which has reached its peak in man, has led, among other things, to a progressive internalization (Hartmann, 1939) and to the development of the instinctual drives; to the organism's readiness to respond to more and more complex stimuli; and to the development of approach apparatuses which *seek and find* adequate stimuli and respond to them. While species-specific behavior patterns ("instincts") are still greatly stimulus-bound in most animals, in man the instinctual drives, as represented by "wishes," are to a considerable extent the motives of behavior.

Eventually, evolution in man resulted in the development of the ego, which became the main "organ of adaptation" (Hartmann, 1939). Once developed, it not only accounted for

[ 138 ]

the execution of wishes, but gradually gave these new content, regulated the energic state of the instinctual drives, and became able to utilize instinctual energy for its own aims (Freud, 1911b; Hartmann, 1939, 1948, 1956a; Loewenstein, 1965). This evolutional and ontogenetic development is to some extent implied in Freud's formulations about the genesis of a wish and of the instinctual drives. Freud described the transition from a primitive mental apparatus, following "the plan of a reflex apparatus," to the development of a "wish," as follows: "the exigencies of life interfere with this simple function, and it is to them, too, that the apparatus owes the impetus to further development. The exigencies of life confront it first in the form of the major somatic needs" (1900, p. 565).

The lines which follow, although previously quoted in the context of the maturational and developmental factors of the id (see Chapter 8), warrant repetition here as essential to the concept pleasure (as distinct from unpleasure) principle:

An essential component of this experience of satisfaction is a particular perception (that of nourishment, in our example) the mnemic image of which remains associated thenceforward with the memory trace of the excitation produced by the need. As a result of the link that has thus been established, next time this need arises a psychical impulse will at once emerge which will seek to re-cathect the mnemic image of the perception and to re-evoke the perception itself, that is to say, to re-establish the situation of the original satisfaction. An impulse of this kind is what we call a *wish;* the reappearance of the perception is the fulfilment of the wish. . . . Thus the aim of this *first psychical activity* was to produce a 'perceptual identity'[1]—a repetition which was linked with the satisfaction of the need.

[1] [I.e. something perceptually identical with the 'experience of satisfaction'.] [1900, pp. 565-566; my italics].

[ 139 ]

Freud's formulation of this development is even more meaningful in his discussion of the genesis of instinctual drives and the differences between organisms operating on the level of a reflex apparatus and those motivated by instinctual drives.

. . . let us assign to the nervous system the task—speaking in general terms—of *mastering stimuli*. We then see how greatly the simple pattern of the physiological reflex is complicated by the introduction of instincts. External stimuli impose only the single task of withdrawing from them; this is accomplished by muscular movements, one of which eventually achieves that aim and thereafter . . . becomes a hereditary disposition. Instinctual stimuli, which originate from within the organism, cannot be dealt with by this mechanism. Thus they make far higher demands on the nervous system and cause it to undertake involved and interconnected activities by which the external world is so changed as to afford satisfaction to the internal source of stimulation. Above all, they oblige the nervous system to renounce its ideal intention of keeping off stimuli, for they maintain an incessant and unavoidable afflux of stimulation. We may therefore well conclude that instincts and not external stimuli are the true motive forces behind the advances that have led the nervous system, with its unlimited capacities, to its present high level of development. There is naturally nothing to prevent our supposing that the instincts themselves are, at least in part, precipitates of the effects of external stimulation, which in the course of phylogenesis have brought about modifications in the living substance [1915a, p. 120].

These formulations of the "wish" and the instinctual drives established the model of an internalized motivational force which in evolutional terms was "the precipitate of external stimulations."[1] According to Freud, as we have seen, the

[1] This formulation, expressed in neo-Lamarckian terms, would have to be brought up to date and expressed in terms of natural selection.

[ 140 ]

memory trace of satisfaction, which is equated with the disappearance of excitation (tension) arising from instinctual demands, is a prerequisite for the formation of a "wish." I postulated earlier that the mnemic image extends early in life not only to the *experience* of satisfaction, but to the total situation[2] which brings it about.

This means that the wish must extend not only to the recathexis of the memory of satisfaction, which Freud equated with the disappearance of unpleasure arising from an upsurge of instinctual demands, but to the recathexis of all the stimuli which are necessary for the achievement of this gratification, and of more and more details of the situation of satisfaction.

*With the emphasis on the wish to recathect the memory of the whole situation, including certain stimuli, it becomes clear that the "constancy" and unpleasure principles cannot apply to this development.* The need to recreate any situation of satisfaction, or at least to recathect its memory trace, is regulated by the *pleasure* principle. The energy behind the wish is represented (given) by the instinctual drives. The pleasure principle regulates the need to seek the object for gratification through approach responses. The approach response, regulated by the pleasure principle, has at least as high a survival value in evolution as the withdrawal response regulated by the unpleasure principle.

I have been considering here Freud's *first* definition of a wish (1900, p. 566) and also his discussion of the instinctual drives in the paragraph quoted from "Instincts and Their Vicissitudes."

However, at the end of the paragraph in which he first gave his definition of "pleasure" and "unpleasure," Freud offered a different definition of "wish." He said that the ac-

---

[2] My use of the term "situation" here is similar to that of Freud in his description of the danger and traumatic situations.

cumulation of excitation was felt as unpleasure and that it "[set] the apparatus in action" to repeat the experience of satisfaction, which involved a diminution of excitation and was felt as pleasure. Freud then stated: *"A current of this kind in the apparatus, starting from unpleasure and aiming at pleasure, we have termed a 'wish' "* (1900, p. 598; my italics).

While Freud was speaking here of "feelings" of pleasure and unpleasure, the whole formulation was an economic one, and the term "current" harked back to the models Freud had used in the "Project" (1895).

This "unpleasure" is also, as Freud later said in *Beyond the Pleasure Principle* (1920, p. 11), "perceptual" unpleasure. In this definition we can detect the model of necessity for withdrawal from excessive external stimulation which was to lead Freud, only two pages later, to the formulation of the unpleasure principle.

Let us now try to bring together the various models thus far discussed which Freud utilized both implicitly and explicitly in describing the development, functioning, and protection of the mental apparatus, and its "regulating principles."

1. The model of a reflex apparatus where external stimuli impose only the single task of withdrawing from them (1915a, p. 120).

2. The "fiction of a primitive psychical apparatus" whose activities are regulated by an effort "to avoid an accumulation of excitation and to maintain itself so far as possible without excitation" (1900, p. 598).

3. The model of a withdrawal reaction to excessive *external* stimulation (1900, p. 600).

4. The model of a "stimulus barrier," which in evolution migrates inward (1920, pp. 27-28).

5. The model of an internalized motivational force which is, in evolutional terms, "the precipitate of external stimulation," and ontogenetically, the result of memory traces of the experience of satisfaction. The concepts of the wish and the instinctual drives follow this model (1900, pp. 565-566; 1915a, pp. 119-120).

We can see that the first three models are all influenced by the constancy principle, and that they emphasize the *necessity* of withdrawing from excessive stimulation in order to prevent tension, which is equated with unpleasure. All in turn are modeled after the automatic (reflex) withdrawal from excessive *external* stimulation, with reference to which Freud coined the term *unpleasure principle.*

It is my contention that the concept *unpleasure principle* applies best to the *necessity* to withdraw from excessive stimulation impinging on the mental apparatus from the outside, where "outside" implies both outside the organism and outside the mental apparatus. Eventually this necessity extends to the withdrawal from the memory traces of such stimulation. The necessity for protection against excessive stimulation is also the basis for Freud's postulation of a protective barrier, which constitutes the fourth model.

It is my further contention that the concept *pleasure principle* applies best to the regulation of the need to recreate any situation of satisfaction, or at least its memory trace; here satisfaction is equated with the disappearance of drive tension. With an accumulating inventory of memory traces, this need will apply to more and more situations of satisfaction.

I must point out here that the term "regulating principle" was understood by Freud, in accordance with Fechner's concept, to be a "tendency" toward stability (1924a, pp. 159-160), and not a mechanism which always resulted in the elimination of all tension.

In order to understand the relationship—which is also a genetic one—between the unpleasure and pleasure principles, and to see how they interact, we must turn once again to Freud's two definitions of a wish, and to the various models he used in formulating the regulatory principles. In both definitions of the wish Freud actually described two phases:

In his *second* definition (1900, p. 598; see Chapter 9 of this monograph), Freud's formulation came closest to the model of Fechner's "tendency towards stability," and also to that of a reflex apparatus—the "fiction of a primitive psychical apparatus." The first stage is represented by an accumulation of excitation, equated with unpleasure. This accumulation of tension then sets the apparatus into action to repeat the situation of satisfaction. The "current" starting from unpleasure and aiming at pleasure Freud calls a wish. He expressed this biphasic formulation even more simply twenty-three years later when he said: "The id, guided by the pleasure principle—that is, by the perception of unpleasure—fends off these tensions in various ways" (1923, p. 47).

These formulations emphasize the *elimination of unpleasure* as the main "aim" of the regulatory principle, and are modeled upon the response to intense external stimulation (danger, fright, pain), the context in which Freud first coined the term *unpleasure principle*. These formulations are expressed mainly in economic terms. If "pleasure" is simply the elimination of "unpleasure," it is understandable that Freud in most instances used the term "pleasure principle," although frequently he did revert to the term "pleasure-unpleasure principle," for example, in a very meaningful paragraph of "The Economic Problem of Masochism" (1924a, pp. 159-160) to which I shall turn later on.

In Freud's *first* definition of a wish (1900, p. 565; see Chapter 9 of this monograph), the biphasic genesis of a wish is described in a more meaningful way. I have already pointed to the evolutional aspect of this formulation and its elaboration in "Instincts and Their Vicissitudes" (1915a, pp. 119-120). Such an evolutional formulation, however, can also be traced to Freud's later statements about the regulatory principles (1920, 1923, and especially 1924a). In Freud's first description of the wish (1900, p. 565) the first phase is represented by the "exigencies of life," the "somatic needs," which in an evolutionally and ontogenetically primitive organism are met by means of a reflex action. In a more advanced organism, this first phase, the "confrontation" with the somatic needs, initiates the second phase, the impulse to produce "something perceptually identical with the 'experience of satisfaction'" (1900, p. 565, n. 1). The wish, then, is the second phase, and presupposes some functioning, albeit primitive, of *perception and memory apparatuses* (see Chapter 3).

With evolution, maturation, and development, this second phase becomes relatively less dependent on external stimulation, and is eventually generated by internalized forces.

We can see that the distinction between the unpleasure and pleasure principles is based on genetic considerations and a recognition of the different models used by Freud. The *unpleasure principle* regulates the elimination of a disturbance of the equilibrium which is equated with unpleasure. It is modeled after excessive external stimulation. It is evolutionally and ontogenetically the more primitive principle.

The *pleasure principle* regulates the need to re-create by action or by fantasy any situation which has created the experience of satisfaction through the elimination of drive tension.[3]

_____

[3] For a discussion of the necessity to distinguish between the concepts pleasure and unpleasure principles and the affects pleasure and unpleasure, see Chapters 11 and 15.

# 14

## The Distinction between the Pleasure and Unpleasure Principles in Freud's Later Work

FREUD'S USE OF various models indicated, if only implicitly, a certain distinction between the pleasure and unpleasure principles. This distinction came closer to an explicit formulation in some of Freud's later works. All such formulations were somewhat obscured, however, by the fact that Freud expressed them within the framework of his dual-instinct theory, in terms of the antithesis between "Thanatos" (death instinct) and "Eros" (libido). This theory in turn made it necessary for Freud to seek new formulations for the regulatory principles.

At this point I shall quote only those paragraphs from Freud's later works which indicate a distinction between the pleasure and unpleasure principles, and leave for later the discussion of such concepts as "repetition compulsion" and "Nirvana" principle, which—at least in Freud's formulations—are inseparable from the death-instinct theory. Such a distinction was expressed in Freud's evaluation of the role of Eros. In *Beyond the Pleasure Principle* the indications of the distinction were of a general nature. In part they were contained in sentences or paragraphs added in later years. Eros was presented in Goethe's terms as the force which "presses forward unsubdued," providing a substitute for the "instinct towards perfection" (1920, pp. 42-43), an instinct the existence of which could not be claimed, according to Freud. In *The Ego and the Id* the role of Eros emerged more distinctly as the disturber of the pleasure principle (which Freud at this juncture equated alternately with the constancy and the Nirvana principles, under the dominance of the death instinct).

> If it is true that Fechner's principle of constancy governs life, which thus consists of a continuous descent towards death, it is the claims of Eros, of the sexual instincts, which, in the form of instinctual needs, hold up the falling level and introduce fresh tensions. The id, guided by the pleasure principle—that is, by the perception of unpleasure— fends off these tensions in various ways [1923, p. 47].

In this paragraph, the pleasure principle is linked with the death instinct and the perception of unpleasure. In accordance with the distinction suggested by me, it would be simpler to say: the unpleasure principle regulates the elimination of tension, while the instinctual drives, represented by wishes, are regulated by the pleasure principle. This simple distinction cannot be made, however, as long as we adhere to the concept of death instinct.

A formulation similar to the one quoted above was made by Freud somewhat further on in the same work:

> It would be possible to picture the id as under the domination of the mute but powerful death instincts, which desire to be at peace and (prompted by the pleasure principle)[1] to put Eros, the mischief-maker, to rest; but perhaps that might be to undervalue the part played by Eros [1923, p. 59].

[1] Here, too, I would use the term unpleasure principle rather than pleasure principle.

In "The Economic Problem of Masochism" (1924a) Freud himself actually suggested a distinction between the pleasure and unpleasure principles, albeit in terms of the life and death instincts.

> . . . we have taken the view that the principle which governs all mental processes is a special case of Fechner's 'tendency towards stability', and have accordingly attributed to the mental apparatus the purpose of reducing to nothing, or at least of keeping as low as possible, the sums of excitation which flow in upon it. Barbara Low . . . has suggested the name of 'Nirvana principle' for this supposed tendency, and we have accepted the term. But we have unhesitatingly identified the pleasure-unpleasure principle with this Nirvana principle. . . . the Nirvana principle (and the pleasure principle which is supposedly identical with it) would be entirely in the service of the death instincts, whose aim is to conduct the restlessness of life into the stability of the inorganic state, and it would have the function of giving warnings against the demands of the life instincts—the libido—which try to disturb the intended course of life.
>
> . . . we must perceive that the Nirvana principle, belonging as it does to the death instinct, has undergone a modification in living organisms through which it has become the pleasure principle; and we shall henceforward avoid regarding the two principles as one. It is not difficult, if we care to follow up this line of thought, to guess what power was the source of the modification. It can only be the life instinct, the libido, which has thus, alongside of the death instinct, seized upon a share in the regulation of the processes of life. In this way we obtain a small but interesting set of connections. The *Nirvana* principle expresses the trend of the death instinct; the *pleasure* principle represents the demands of the libido [1924a, pp. 159-160].

If we substitute the term "unpleasure principle" for the term "Nirvana principle," which, as Freud distinctly said, is inseparable from his death-instinct theory; if we look upon

[ 148 ]

what Freud called "the modification in living organisms" in evolutional and ontogenetic terms, we arrive at the distinction between the unpleasure and pleasure principles suggested by me.

I am aware of the fact that the postulate suggested above demands a discussion of such thorny topics as: What is "beyond the pleasure principle"? What is the meaning of the repetition compulsion? What is the significance of the death-instinct concept? Before undertaking this, I must point out the similarities and differences between the forms of tension reduction resulting from behavior regulated by the unpleasure principle and those regulated by the pleasure principle.

Certain biological and evolutional considerations are essential here. I have already mentioned that the withdrawal from a too-intense stimulus, in contrast to the approach toward a low-grade stimulus, is one of the two basic biological response patterns. These antithetic responses can be traced throughout the evolutionary series. Freud (1900, p. 600) used the response to what he called "the experience of an external fright"[2] as the prime example of regulation through the unpleasure principle, and as the model for defense. The biological response of withdrawal has, of course, eminent survival value. In the course of evolution, withdrawal becomes more species specific and selective. This selectivity may be transmitted by the genetic code, but some animals have to acquire it by habituation (Thorpe, 1956; Schur, 1961a).[3] With the development of certain analogues of psychic structure, withdrawal develops into the response of avoidance, which is a psychological concept, in contrast to the biophysiological concept of withdrawal. Enlarging upon Freud's formulation,

[2] We would now say: "external danger."

[3] The innate species-specific selectivity of responses to danger has been conceptualized by the ethologists as innate releasing mechanisms (IRMs). Such selectivity can also be understood in terms of internalization (Hartmann).

it seems legitimate to assume not only that the unpleasure principle regulates the necessity to withdraw from the source of pain (danger), but that such a regulatory mechanism which I have tried to conceptualize in psychological terms as the unpleasure principle has developed in evolution because this necessity of withdrawing from excessive stimulation has adaptive (survival) value.

The necessity to withdraw from "unpleasure"—represented by excessive external stimulation—is part of the innate endowment, gains mental representation, and eventually is manifested in all structures.

An additional reason for the distinction between the pleasure and unpleasure principles is the following consideration: Freud himself formulated the distinction between the demands of the instinctual drives and the response to external danger. As previously quoted, he said in "Instincts and Their Vicissitudes": "External stimuli impose only the single task of withdrawing from them; . . . Instinctual stimuli, which originate from within the organism, cannot be dealt with by this mechanism. . . . they cause it [the nervous system] to undertake . . . activities by which the external world is so changed as to afford satisfaction to the internal source of stimulation" (1915a, p. 120).

It is clear, therefore, that the instinctual drives—and the wishes expressing them—press for discharge through the establishment of "perceptual identity" (Freud, 1900, pp. 565-566, 602). This process is regulated by the pleasure principle. The experience of pain (excessive stimulation, later danger) stimulates withdrawal[4] and is regulated by the unpleasure principle. In normal circumstances there is no wish to discharge the responses—if the source of unpleasure (later danger) is eliminated (see also Schur, 1960a). Masochism and

[4] Avoidance is not an automatic response but a function of the ego under the influence of the secondary process.

[ 150 ]

neurotic tension pleasure (Schur, 1963) are much later and much more complex acquisitions.

This is an important additional reason for distinguishing between the pleasure and unpleasure principles. The development of instinctual drives as they exist in man is one of the aspects of evolution. *The need to withdraw from the source of pain and danger has not achieved in the course of evolution the degree of internalization which is the basis for an instinctual drive.* There is no motivational force to *seek* an object in order to withdraw from it. *We therefore cannot speak of an "instinctual drive" to withdraw from pain and danger.* (For the opposite view, see Brunswick, 1954.)[5] There is only a propensity to respond to certain stimuli with withdrawal and certain species-specific discharge patterns. This

[5] Robert W. White (1963, pp. 154-156) scathingly criticizes Freud's "failure" to assign to anxiety the status of an "instinct." This is not the place for an exhaustive discussion of White's critique (see Rapaport, 1960a) and only some points can be raised here.

1. When White says, in accordance with MacDougall, that in view of "the importance of fear in overt animal and human behavior, . . . it seemed obvious to postulate a fear instinct," he is falling into the trap of equating the concept "instinct" of the ethologists and some biologists with Freud's concept of instinctual drives.

2. Freud, in *Inhibitions, Symptoms and Anxiety,* not only discussed signal anxiety, which signals danger, but dealt with the genetic aspect of anxiety, which links this response to the physiological precursors of the affect anxiety.

3. White puts too much emphasis on certain metaphors and anthropomorphic formulations used by Freud in *Inhibitions, Symptoms and Anxiety* (Schur, 1953, 1955, 1960a.).

4. Most animals have developed through evolution certain IRMs and species-specific response patterns to "dangerous" stimuli. However, White should be aware that a good many contemporary American students of animal behavior frown upon the whole "instinct" concept (Schneirla, 1956; Lehrman, 1961).

5. Freud modeled the anxiety response upon the reaction to excessive external stimulation as far back as 1900 (p. 600). It was this model which led me in the first place to suggest the distinction between the pleasure and unpleasure principles.

6. While Freud discussed "signal anxiety" mainly in the context of "inner," "instinctual" danger, because of its importance for neurosogenesis and symptom formation, he never neglected the external, environmental source of danger.

[ 151 ]

response is the model both for the anxiety response and for defense (Freud [1900, p. 600] spoke of primary repression), and it is regulated by the unpleasure principle. We usually assume that both the gratification of a wish (using this term as discussed by me) and the disappearance of pain-danger result in tension reduction. It seems justified to assume, however, that there are differences in the tension reduction in the two circumstances, both on the neurophysiological[6] and the psychological (economic, structural, experiential) levels.[7] This difference becomes quite obvious, especially in normal development. The development of many ego structures is required before the *need* to withdraw from danger (pain) develops into a *wish* to avoid danger. We can speculate, however, that the precursors of such wishes are autonomous and may also come under the influence of the pleasure and unpleasure principles.

---

[6] See, for example, the experiments by Lilly (1960).

[7] On the experiential level there is in most instances a great difference between the *feeling* of relief following the disappearance of tension (pain, danger, etc.) and the *feeling* of satisfaction, pleasure, joy, etc., following the gratification of an instinctual wish. This belongs, however, to a discussion of the distinction between the affects pleasure and unpleasure, which I shall take up in Chapter 15.

# 15

## *"Beyond the Pleasure Principle" and the Repetition Compulsion*

M<small>Y</small> DISCUSSION could actually have ended at this point if we were concerned only with the pleasure and unpleasure principles. If, however, we seek clarification of the various concepts of superordinated regulatory principles formulated by Freud, we must examine at least some of the new concepts introduced by him in 1920.

*Beyond the Pleasure Principle* is a *tour de force* in which Freud first conceptualized aggression—encountered in all its ramifications in his daily work with patients, in dreams, in his observations of the oedipus complex—as a separate instinctual drive, thereby introducing the dual-instinct theory. However, this work also contains a series of speculations which have been haunting psychoanalytic literature since 1920, and have become the source of endless controversy as well as the topic of many panel discussions. I neither contemplate reviewing here *all* the literature on the death-instinct theory, nor do I consider this to be necessary. My discussion will be limited (and even this limited goal is far from easy) to the following points:

1. I shall attempt to explain within the framework of the unpleasure-pleasure principles certain phenomena which Freud designated as "beyond the pleasure principle."

2. I shall therefore dispute the necessity for postulating a

Nirvana principle. Above all, however, I shall question the assumption according to which the repetition compulsion is assigned the role of regulatory principle overriding all the others (unpleasure, pleasure, reality principles).

In the Postscript to his *Autobiographical Study*, added in 1935, Freud said:

> I have never ceased my analytic work nor my writing. . . . But I myself find that a significant change has come about. Threads which in the course of my development had become intertangled have now begun to separate; interests which I had acquired in the later part of my life have receded, while the older and original ones become prominent once more. . . . My interest, after making a lifelong *detour* through the natural sciences, medicine and psychotherapy, returned to the cultural problems which had fascinated me long before, when I was a youth scarcely old enough for thinking [pp. 71-72].

While Freud had every reason to consider *Beyond the Pleasure Principle* as a work which dealt with basic problems of the working of the mind—and beyond that, of all natural sciences—he was the first to admit that he had given free rein in this book to "speculation, often far-fetched speculation" (p. 24). He ended the book with a kind of confession:

> It may be asked whether and how far I am myself convinced of the truth of the hypotheses that have been set out in these pages. My answer would be that I am not convinced myself and that I do not seek to persuade other people to believe in them. . . . There is no reason, as it seems to me, why the emotional factor of conviction should enter into this question at all. It is surely possible to throw oneself into a line of thought and to follow it wherever it leads out of simple scientific curiosity, or, if the reader prefers, as an *advocatus diaboli,* who is not on that account himself sold to the devil. I do not dispute the fact that the

third step in the theory of the instincts, which I have taken here, cannot lay claim to the same degree of certainty as the two earlier ones—the extension of the concept of sexuality and the hypothesis of narcissism. These two innovations were a direct translation of observation into theory and were no more open to sources of error than is inevitable in all such cases. It is true that my assertion of the regressive character of instincts also rests upon observed material—namely on the facts of the compulsion to repeat. It may be, however, that I have overestimated their significance. And in any case it is impossible to pursue an idea of this kind except by repeatedly combining factual material with what is purely speculative and thus diverging widely from empirical observation. The more frequently this is done in the course of constructing a theory, the more untrustworthy, as we know, must be the final result. But the degree of uncertainty is not assignable. *One may have made a lucky hit or one may have gone shamefully astray* [p. 59; my italics].[1]

However, Freud did base his "far-fetched speculations" on a series of valid empirical observations. Thus the question can only be whether Freud's constructs are as valid as his observations, and are necessary for their explanation.

Freud reaffirmed the view expressed in earlier works (see Chapter 9) that his concept of the pleasure principle was based on the constancy principle, the endeavor of the mental apparatus

. . . to keep the quantity of excitation present in it as low as possible, or at least to keep it constant. This latter hypothesis is only another way of stating the pleasure principle; for if the work of the mental apparatus is directed towards keeping the quantity of excitation low, then anything that is calculated to increase that quantity is bound to be felt as adverse to the functioning of the apparatus,

1 For a discussion of Freud's formulation of the death-instinct theory, see footnote 20 in this chapter.

that is, as unpleasurable. The pleasure principle follows from the principle of constancy: actually the latter principle was inferred from the facts which forced us to adopt the pleasure principle.

[Freud then added an important restriction:] It must be pointed out, however, that strictly speaking it is incorrect to talk of the dominance of the pleasure principle over the course of mental processes. If such a dominance existed, the immense majority of our mental processes would have to be accompanied by pleasure or to lead to pleasure, whereas universal experience completely contradicts any such conclusion. The most that can be said, therefore, is that there exists in the mind a strong *tendency* towards the pleasure principle, but that that tendency is opposed by certain other forces or circumstances, so that the final outcome cannot always be in harmony with the tendency towards pleasure. We may compare what Fechner (1873, 90) remarks on a similar point: 'Since however a tendency towards an aim does not imply that the aim is attained, and since in general the aim is attainable only by approximations . . .' [pp. 9-10].[2]

This restriction of a "regulating principle" to a "tendency" or an "attempt" has, of course, *general* validity. It applies not only to "drives" and "wishes" but to species-specific behavior patterns, frequently described as "instincts" or "instinctive," which have been laid down in the course of evolution because of their eminent survival value. Many of them may misfire and lead to the extinction of the phenotype or even of a whole species in a changed ecological environment.

We see in the above-quoted paragraph and the subsequent discussion one fundamental difficulty; Freud's original formu-

[2] It is pertinent that Freud used a similar formulation when he discussed the wish fulfillment of dreams in his *New Introductory Lectures:* "We say that a dream is the fulfilment of a wish; but if you want to take these latter objections [that in cases of traumatic neuroses dreams regularly end in the generation of anxiety] into account, you can say nevertheless that a dream is an *attempt* at the fulfilment of a wish" (1933, p. 29).

lation of the unpleasure-pleasure regulatory principles was expressed on the one hand in biological (neurophysiological) terms, and on the other hand—to the extent that he used a metapsychological framework—mainly in economic terms: increase of tension = unpleasure; decrease of tension (re-establishment of an equilibrium) = pleasure. Yet in that part of *Beyond the Pleasure Principle* in which Freud tried to sub-stantiate his main concepts, he used "pleasure" and "unpleas-ure" chiefly in terms of an experience or an affect, although returning again and again to a biopsychological, economic frame of reference. Moreover, Freud stated that "most of the unpleasure we experience is perceptual unpleasure" (1920, p. 11); and he had also recognized as far back as *The Interpreta-tion of Dreams* that wish fulfillment in dreams did not, in most instances, arouse pleasurable feelings. He had explained both in the *Introductory Lectures* (1916-1917) and in a 1919 footnote appended to *The Interpretation of Dreams* (1900, pp. 580-581)—illustrating his point with the fairy tale about the three wishes—that when we consider wish fulfillment we must always ask ourselves: "Who is experiencing pleasure?"

At this point, though, Freud had not yet arrived at the structural formulations of affects which he later developed in *Inhibitions, Symptoms and Anxiety* (1926).[3] The unpleasure-constancy-Nirvana-pleasure principles are basically economic regulatory principles dealing with the accumulation and avoidance of tension and also with the seeking of stimuli and objects for discharge of tension. The *affects* pleasure and un-pleasure are—like all affects—complex ego responses with many genetically determined, hierarchical layers. They are dependent upon the state of all three structures and on the relationship of these to the environment. This difference be-tween the affects pleasure and unpleasure and the pleasure-

[3] See also Freud's footnote added to *Beyond the Pleasure Principle* (1920, p. 11) in 1925.

unpleasure principles has frequently been overlooked or at least not sufficiently stressed, unfortunately even by Freud (Jacobson, 1953; Lipin, 1963; on the other hand, see Rapaport, 1960a).

Let us examine the situations which Freud considered either as an inhibition of or as a "breach" in the pleasure principle, or else as *beyond* that principle.

1. According to Freud, the transition from the pleasure principle to the reality principle (1911b, 1920, p. 10; Hartmann, 1939, 1956a) represented an *inhibition* of the pleasure principle. *Delay* produced, in economic terms, a temporary increase of tension. It guaranteed the avoidance of danger, however, and an eventual *experience* of pleasure of a different order. Here we can already detect the hierarchical formulation of the affect pleasure, which can be derived from something other than a *direct* satisfaction of an instinctual demand.

2. Freud's example of a *"breach"* in the pleasure principle refers to maturational and developmental aspects of the "mental apparatus" of both the id and the ego, which lead to intrasystemic and intersystemic conflicts, and hence to experiences of unpleasure instead of pleasure (1920, p. 11). (See also Hartmann's formulations about such conflicts [1939, 1964]; Loewenstein [1965].[4])

3. Freud then proceeded to other examples which he no longer considered an inhibition or a breach of the pleasure principle, but proof of some other principle "beyond" the latter. Such examples were:

a. The dreams occurring in "traumatic neuroses," in which the patient repeats the traumatic situation.

b. Certain types of children's play, especially the reel and

4 Lipin's paper on "The Repetition Compulsion and 'Maturational' Drive-Representatives" (1963) deals in detail with the vicissitudes of those drive derivatives which have never reached satisfaction (see footnote 24 in this chapter).

peek-a-boo games which Freud had observed in his grandson. For these, however, he still, at least initially, conceded the possibility of an explanation "within" the pleasure principle.

c. The compulsion of patients in analysis to repeat painful experiences of their past, especially of their early childhood, a phenomenon which Freud described as transference neurosis. Freud made two significant statements in this context: first, that "the greater part of what is re-experienced under the compulsion to repeat[5] must cause the ego unpleasure, since it brings to light activities of repressed instinctual impulses. That, however, is unpleasure of a kind we have already considered and does not contradict the pleasure principle: unpleasure for one system and simultaneously satisfaction for the other" (p. 20).

He then added a second statement which actually committed him to the assumption that the repetition compulsion was beyond the pleasure principle: "we come now to a new and remarkable fact, namely that the compulsion to repeat also recalls from the past experiences which include no possibility of pleasure, and which can never, even long ago, have brought satisfaction even to instinctual impulses which have since been repressed" (p. 20).

Here pleasure and unpleasure have been considered exclusively in experiential terms. Freud's doubts are exemplified by a sentence which he added in 1921: "They [the various repetitions of painful, frustrating experiences] are of course the activities of instincts [instinctual drives] intended to lead to satisfaction; but no lesson has been learnt from the old experi-

---

5 The distinction between "compulsion to repeat" and "repetition compulsion" gets lost, unfortunately, in Strachey's translation of the German word *Wiederholungszwang*. The term "compulsion to repeat" is used throughout without an editorial note explaining the distinction between these two concepts. There is a basic difference between the empirically valid observation of a compulsion to repeat and the theoretical concept of a repetition compulsion as an overriding regulatory principle of mental functioning.

ence of these activities having led instead only to unpleasure" (p. 21).

4. The phenomenon Freud called the fate neurosis, the behavior of people which leads them from one tragedy to another and gives them the impression of "being pursued by a malignant fate or possessed by some 'daemonic' power" (p. 21). It is puzzling that Freud should have introduced this example with the statement: "What psycho-analysis reveals in the transference phenomena of neurotics can also be observed in the lives of some *normal* people" (my italics).

A further allusion to fate is made in the following sentences:

We are much more impressed by cases where the subject appears to have a *passive* experience, over which he has no influence, but in which he meets with a repetition of the same fatality. There is the case, for instance, of the woman who married three successive husbands each of whom fell ill soon afterwards and had to be nursed by her on their death-beds. The most moving poetic picture of a fate such as this is given by Tasso in his romantic epic *Gerusalemme Liberata*. Its hero, Tancred, unwittingly kills his beloved Clorinda in a duel while she is disguised in the armour of an enemy knight. After her burial he makes his way into a strange magic forest which strikes the Crusaders' army with terror. He slashes with his sword at a tall tree; but blood streams from the cut and the voice of Clorinda, whose soul is imprisoned in the tree, is heard complaining that he has wounded his beloved once again [p. 22].

Freud then returned to the example of traumatic neurosis, which formed the main pillar of his thesis, and after an extensive metapsychological discussion of the stimulus barrier and the consequences of its being breached, he made a final statement about posttraumatic dreams and certain dreams which occur during psychoanalysis, not without again expressing mental reservations about the latter.

This would seem to be the place, then, at which to admit for the first time an exception to the proposition that dreams are fulfilments of wishes. Anxiety dreams, as I have shown repeatedly and in detail, offer no such exception. Nor do 'punishment' dreams, for they merely replace the forbidden wish-fulfilment by the appropriate punishment for it; that is to say, they fulfil the wish of the sense of guilt which is the reaction to the repudiated impulse. But it is impossible to classify as wish-fulfilments the dreams we have been discussing which occur in traumatic neuroses, or the dreams during psycho-analysis which bring to memory the psychical traumas of childhood. They arise, rather, in obedience to the compulsion to repeat, though it is true that in analysis that compulsion is supported by the wish (which is encouraged by 'suggestion') to conjure up what has been forgotten and repressed [p. 32].

After committing himself to the "daemonic" aspect of the compulsion to repeat, Freud tried to provide an explanation which finally led to his new theory of "instincts."

. . . how is the predicate of being 'instinctual' [*das Trieb-hafte*] related to the compulsion to repeat? At this point we cannot escape a suspicion that we may have come upon the track of a universal attribute of instincts and perhaps of organic life in general which has not hitherto been clearly recognized or at least not explicitly stressed. *It seems, then, that an instinct [Trieb] is an urge inherent in organic life to restore an earlier state of things* which the living entity has been obliged to abandon under the pressure of external disturbing forces; that is, it is a kind of organic elasticity or, to put it another way, the expression of the inertia inherent in organic life [p. 36].

In this context the translation of the term *Trieb* by "in-stinct" rather than "instinctual drive" is somewhat more accurate since, as we shall see, this definition of Freud's and his whole elaboration of it has many roots in the "instinct" concept used by biologists.[6]

Once Freud had taken this step, the logical inference was that:

It would be in contradiction to the conservative nature of the instincts if the goal of life were a state of things which had never yet been attained. On the contrary, it must be an *old* state of things, an initial state from which the living entity has at one time or other departed and to which it is striving to return by the circuitous paths along which its development leads. If we are to take it as a truth that knows no exception that everything living dies for *internal* reasons—becomes inorganic once again—then we shall be compelled to say that '*the aim of all life is death*' and, looking backwards, that '*inanimate things existed before living ones*' [p. 38].

It was also logical for Freud to belittle the importance of the "instincts" of self preservation, self assertion, and mastery.

The implications in regard to the great groups of instincts which, as we believe, lie behind the phenomena of life in organisms must appear no less bewildering. The hypothesis of self-preservative instincts, such as we attribute to all living beings, stands in marked opposition to the idea that instinctual life as a whole serves to bring about death. Seen in this light, the theoretical importance of the instincts of self-preservation, of self-assertion and of mastery greatly diminishes.[7] They are component instincts whose function it is to assure that the organism shall follow its own path to death, and to ward off any possible ways of returning to inorganic existence other than those which are immanent

[6] However, the term "instinct" as used by ethologists, for example, comprises both the "drive element" or an instinct and the resulting species-specific behavior pattern.

[7] While Freud frequently used the concept of an "instinct of self-preservation," the attribution of the term "instinct" to "self-assertion" and "mastery" had not been made by him before this point, to the best of my knowledge.

in the organism itself. We have no longer to reckon with the organism's puzzling determination (so hard to fit into any context) to maintain its own existence in the face of every obstacle. *What we are left with is the fact that the organism wishes to die only in its own fashion.* Thus these guardians of life, too, were originally the myrmidons of death. Hence arises the paradoxical situation that the living organism struggles most energetically against events (dangers, in fact) which might help it to attain its life's aim rapidly—by a kind of short-circuit. Such behavior is, however, precisely what characterizes purely instinctual as contrasted with intelligent efforts [p. 39; my italics].

At this point Freud, however, had to recoil from this extreme position, and say:

> *But let us pause for a moment and reflect. It cannot be so. The sexual instincts, to which the theory of the neuroses gives a quite special place, appear under a very different aspect* [p. 39; my italics].

For this aspect, which was essential for the preservation of a theory of dual instinctual drives, Freud found support in the special role of the germ cell (the germ plasm). He was following here the theories of A. Weismann, who, as Freud put it, had "introduced the division of living substance into mortal and immortal parts" (1920, p. 45).

> [The germ cells] probably retain the original structure of living matter and, after a certain time, with their full complement of inherited and freshly acquired instinctual dispositions, separate themselves from the organism as a whole. These two characteristics may be precisely what enables them to have an independent existence. Under favourable conditions, they begin to develop—that is, to repeat the performance to which they owe their existence. . . .[8] These

---

[8] This role of the germ cells would now be expressed in terms of the genetic code.

germ-cells, therefore, work against the death of the living substance and succeed in winning for it what we can only regard as potential immortality, though that may mean no more than a lengthening of the road to death. . . .

The instincts which watch over the destinies of these elementary organisms that survive the whole individual, which provide them with a safe shelter while they are defenseless against the stimuli of the external world, which bring about their meeting with other germ-cells, and so on—these constitute the group of the sexual instincts. They are conservative in the same sense as the other instincts in that they bring back earlier states of living substance; but they are conservative to a higher degree in that they are peculiarly resistant to external influences; and they are conservative too in another sense in that they preserve life itself for a comparatively long period. They are the true life instincts [p. 40].

Freud turned to such biologists as Weismann and Woodruff, not so much for proof that his hypothesis of the death instinct was correct, but to ascertain whether his "expectation that biology would flatly contradict the recognition of death instincts" had been fulfilled. He found that it had not,[9] with the result that: "We are at liberty to continue concerning ourselves with their possibility, if we have other reasons for doing so" (p. 49).

On the other hand, he found in the work of Weismann and in Hering's theory of the two antagonistic processes at work in living substance—the constructive or assimilatory and the destructive or dissimilatory—a confirmation of his theory of *dual* instinctual drives. Freud even found himself, albeit reluctantly, in "the harbour of Schopenhauer's philosophy," which asserted that "death is the 'true result and to that extent the purpose of life', while the sexual instinct is the embodiment of the will to live" (p. 50).

9 See footnote 11 in Chapter 4.

This discussion is concerned with Freud's death-instinct theory mainly because of the latter's inseparable link with his formulations on the regulatory principles.

I have already quoted Freud's new definition of an instinct as an urge inherent in organic life toward restoring an earlier state of things. This definition was repeated in an intrinsically identical form in connection with the regulatory principles, when Freud said:

> The dominating tendency of mental life, and perhaps of nervous life in general, is the effort to reduce, to keep constant or to remove internal tension due to stimuli (the 'Nirvana principle', to borrow a term from Barbara Low . . .)—a tendency which finds expression in the pleasure principle; and our recognition of that fact is one of our strongest reasons for believing in the existence of death instincts [pp. 55-56].

He then added that the repetition compulsion had first put him on the track of the death instinct. The constancy-Nirvana-pleasure and repetition-compulsion principles were then taken as proof of the death-instinct concept, which in turn was used as an explanation for these same principles.

In order to complete the *dual* aspect of his theory of instinctual drives, on the one hand, and to establish the link between the sexual instinctual drive and the repetition compulsion as a superordinated compulsion to repeat, on the other, Freud turned first to biology for support. It is interesting that this is the only time, as far as I know, that Freud referred to the import of the concept of survival value in Darwin's theory of evolution—using the expression "*sober* Darwinian lines" (p. 56; my italics).

To be able to trace the need to restore an earlier state of things in the sexual instinctual drive as well, Freud had to turn—to Plato's *Symposium* and to the *Upanishads*! (See footnote 27 in this chapter.)

It was necessary to outline Freud's far-fetched speculations before I could dispute: (a) the validity of his adjudging certain behavioral phenomena to be beyond the pleasure-unpleasure principles as these were originally formulated by Freud and then somewhat modified by me; and (b) the validity of his conceiving of the repetition compulsion as an overriding regulatory principle, as distinguished from the compulsion to repeat which permits of a different explanation, a concept which was inseparable not only from his death-instinct theory, but from his new general definition of an instinct as "an urge inherent in organic life to restore an earlier state of things."

If we examine all the examples offered by Freud as proof of the existence of some "daemonic" power—posttraumatic dreams, children's play, the behavior of patients in the psychoanalytic situation and in the fate neurosis—we find one common denominator: the repetitiveness of all physiological functioning and of behavior. Repetitiveness is transmitted to every living structure—animal and plant—by the genetic code, in a manner which is the outcome of evolution. It manifests itself as much, for example, in the physiological aspect of the dream cycles as in the functioning of all psychic structures. *Evolution has resulted in the development of psychic structures which enable man to tend to avoid a rigid repetitiveness of behavior. The ego, the organ of adaptation, is such a structure, and the success of this tendency depends on the degree of ego autonomy attained* (Hartmann, 1939, 1964). However, even this very tendency to *escape* repetitiveness generally shows certain repetitive characteristics.[10] Freud himself emphasized throughout his work—whether he was using topographic or structural terms—that unconscious wishes

[10] For other manifestations of repetitiveness, see, among others, Hartmann's discussion of "preconscious automatism" (1939).

"share this character of indestructibility with all other mental acts which are truly unconscious. . . . These are paths which have been laid down once and for all, which never fall into disuse and which, whenever an unconscious excitation re-cathects them, are always ready to conduct the excitatory process to discharge" (1900, p. 553, n. 1). He pointed out that the id and its contents were "virtually immortal" (1933, p. 74). Before formulating the structural theory, he described the "compulsion to repeat" as characteristic of the "unconscious" or of the operation of the instinctual drives (1915a).

Freud stated again and again that infantile instinctual demands which have not found gratification press for discharge. This assumption, of the incessant recurrence of unfulfilled wishes, is one of the cornerstones of Freud's theory regarding such mental phenomena as dreams and neurotic symptom formation.

While Freud thus recognized and conceptualized the tendency to repetitiveness as characteristic of instinctual demands, he seems to have been puzzled by other, similar characteristics of behavior, or, in structural terms, by certain aspects of ego and superego functioning.

We are faced here with a certain paradox: it was Freud who discovered the ubiquitous mental phenomenon which he described in 1900 as the "dream work"—a compromise formation of unconscious wishes and preconscious day residue, distorted by the influence of censorship. (We speak today of a compromise among the three structures: id, ego, and superego.) In 1926 Freud formulated the concept of "signal anxiety," which is an *ego* response to awareness of external or instinctual danger; he described the shift of cathexes, resulting in a reinforcement of defenses—another ego function; he characterized as "the riddle of neurosis" (also in 1926) the fact that dangers which are realistic enough at various stages of infancy never lose their aspect of psychic reality. And while

[ 167 ]

Freud spoke of the riddle of *neurosis,* we know that all these mechanisms are ubiquitous in varying degrees, influencing our behavior to a greater or lesser extent. It was Freud who spoke in his *Introductory Lectures* about the blow to our narcissism inflicted by what was then the latest scientific revolution—the psychological one[11]—which was proving that man was not even master in his own house (1916-1917, pp. 284-285). And yet, in *Beyond the Pleasure Principle,* Freud felt compelled to engage in the far-reaching speculations we have indicated. We must ask ourselves the following questions:

1. Is the attribute "daemonic" appropriate to the characteristic of repetitiveness?

2. Does repetitiveness—which manifests itself in the functioning of all psychic structures—justify the assumption that an instinct is an "urge inherent in organic life to restore an *earlier* state of things"?

3. Finally, do the various manifestations of repetitiveness contradict the concepts of the unpleasure and pleasure principles?

Such concepts as the universe (both the macrocosm and the microcosm) and the facts we know about it—the beginning of life on this planet, life's evolutional development, the working of the genetic code, the forces operating within the atom —have something awe-inspiring about them. And this applies as well to behavior motivated by instinctual drives and to such species-specific behavior patterns as are called "instinctive." However, we must distinguish between "awe-inspiring" and "daemonic." Freud used the attribute "daemonic" to describe those motivational forces which lead to behavior causing frustration, unhappiness, often tragedy. In other words, Freud was concerned in this instance with the *con-*

11 Freud was later obliged to recognize that the "atomic" revolution represented a new phase in the "breakdown of today's Weltanschauung." (See his exchange of letters with Marie Bonaparte [in Schur, 1965a].)

*sequences* and not with the forces at work, and he then deduced his theory about these forces from their consequences.

Repetitiveness in the macrocosm, the formation and destruction of stars, or even galaxies, are probably beyond the comprehension even of astronomers. But *we* are concerned with the microcosm. Repetitiveness is one of the basic characteristics of all physiological functioning and of behavior. When we seek *causes* for the fact that in our part of the world, on a hot, humid night, the air in wooded areas, adjacent to stagnant water, is filled with myriads of tiny insects which, attracted by light, pass through every screen, we find them in the insects' species-specific response pattern to certain stimuli. When the next morning we find screens and window panes covered by masses of dead insects, we may be awed by the backfiring of certain behavior patterns, which nevertheless must have developed in the course of evolution because they had a high survival value. *However, the tragic fact that such patterns, instead of serving survival, end in the destruction of the phenotype, does not denote the presence of an instinct whose aim it would be to achieve this fatal goal.*

We may think that the distinction between such attributes as "daemonic" and "awe-inspiring" is an exercise in semantics. It is evident, however, that the repetitiveness of painful dreams and experiences which Freud characterized as daemonic is a necessary stepping stone toward his new general formulation of "instincts," more specifically, the "death instinct," as well as of the repetition compulsion. We cannot escape the conclusion that Freud had already arrived at his ultimate hypothesis of the death instinct (Schur, 1966) and was using the various aspects of "unpleasurable" repetitiveness to confirm it, while at the same time using this hypothesis as an explanation of the phenomena he had observed.

In his new definition of an instinct Freud departed from some of the basic attributes he had assigned to the instinctual

[ 169 ]

drives (1915a), e.g., the *aim* of finding an *object* for their discharge.

On the one hand, Freud's new definition, the examples chosen from biology—the migration of fish (salmon) at spawning time, the migratory flights of birds—and the discussion of the "instincts" of "self-preservation" and of "mastery" all utilized the term *"Trieb"* in the same way as biologists would use the term "instinct."[12] The latter always includes the concept of a species-specific behavior pattern and not just that of a motivational force, which is what Freud's general use of the term *"Trieb"* signified.

On the other hand, Freud based this new definition of "instincts" on *his* interpretation of the constancy (Nirvana) principle, which has nothing in common with the biological concept of instinct. Ethologists who use the concept "instinct" widely (Tinbergen, 1951; Lorenz, 1964), as well as other students of animal behavior, view species-specific behavior patterns as the result of evolution, which "preserves" such functions and the organs necessary for their execution, because under specific ecological conditions they have eminent survival value for the species. This also applies, of course, to those mutations which account for the development of new functions, organs, and eventually species. Repetitiveness of physiological responses and behavior is rooted in the genetic code, which directs growth and maturation of the phenotype and also the general type of response to certain environmental stimuli. It is entirely conceivable that the genetic code is also capable of bringing about the formation of certain systems of functions (for example, enzymes; see Chapter 4, footnote 11) which act against the survival of the phenotype. However,

12 We know, of course, that fish and birds do not migrate back to certain areas because they want to return to their place of birth, but because they respond to certain perceptual stimuli in a species-specific pattern. No biologist acknowledges the existence of an "instinct" of self preservation or of a "maternal instinct."

[ 170 ]

calling such functions—if they exist—"urges," and hence "instincts," which would influence specific forms of behavior, is a speculation which so far cannot be proven.

Freud was on much firmer ground, however, when he saw in a stereotyped repetitiveness a more primitive manifestation of mental functioning. In the examples he gave we see not only the manifestation of the instinctual drives which seek for discharge in a repetitive way. Every type of behavior also depends on the functional state of the executive apparatus. In the transference neurosis, in the fate neurosis, in severe obsessive-compulsive states, in posttraumatic states, the ego has lost those faculties which guarantee autonomy from the environment and freedom from domination by the instinctual drives, along with an ability to maintain a wide range of responses. Such stereotyped repetitive behavior is then closer to the species-specific (instinctive) behavior patterns of animals (see Chapter 16).

The last question to be answered is whether the various manifestations of repetitiveness contradict the pleasure-unpleasure principles.

At the risk of being "repetitive," I must return to the basic difficulty inherent in Freud's reasoning which led him "beyond" the pleasure principle (see Chapter 9). It is a long way from pleasure-unpleasure as regulating principles to pleasure-unpleasure as affects. The principles have been conceptualized as describing the *tendency* to avoid the accumulation of tension which can arise from excessive internal or external stimulation. Excessive internal tension initiates the tendency to seek an object for drive discharge; excessive external stimulation initiates the tendency to withdraw from the source of the stimulation. Both responses result in the re-establishment of an equilibrium. The tendency to seek such gratification of wishes and avoid excessive stimulation is not limited to the discharge of instinctual drives, but eventually manifests itself

[ 171 ]

in an increasingly complex hierarchy of wishes representing the demands of the ego and superego. The pleasure and unpleasure principles will therefore also regulate a *tendency* toward interstructural equilibrium, which in turn also presupposes an equilibrium between the self and the object world (see Hartmann, 1939; Jacobson, 1964). However, these regulatory principles cannot guarantee the achievement or avoidance of the *affects* pleasure and unpleasure. Wishes which are influenced by derivatives of libidinal or aggressive drive components clash with the "reality principle," which represents the influence of the other structures and the environment. Wishes arising under the dominance of the ego and superego, and influenced by the reality principle, result in delay or renunciation of instinctual gratification. Unpleasurable affects can therefore arise from gratification of conscious, or more frequently unconscious, instinctual wishes.

We could assume that all this was commonplace, and therefore not in need of extensive discussion, were the concept of "beyond the pleasure principle" not so widely accepted in psychoanalytic literature, even by authors who do not express agreement with the death-instinct theory.

Let us examine the examples which Freud considered to be proof of his assumption that there exists a "beyond the pleasure principle," or rather which he viewed as contradictions of the pleasure-unpleasure principles. He began and ended his argument with what he considered to be his most valid example—the posttraumatic dream, which has "the characteristic of repeatedly bringing the patient back into the situation of his accident, a situation from which he wakes up in another fright" (p. 13). Let us therefore consider Freud's examples in the order of the validity he ascribed to them as proof of his theories: posttraumatic dreams, the behavior of patients in analysis, the fate neurosis, the play of children.

We need touch only tangentially upon his examples drawn from biology.

Freud emphasized correctly that the causation of traumatic neuroses occurring after accidents is linked with the factor of surprise, the lack of preparedness for danger, hence the resultant anxiety reaction. It is well known that the details of many such accidents, especially the cases of "shellshock" during World War I, were frequently obscured by a posttraumatic amnesia, even in the absence of any "organic" damage, such as concussion. This element of surprise and unpreparedness applies also to car and train accidents.[13]

Posttraumatic amnesia was also quite common, however, in the acute, psychosislike states observed so frequently in soldiers during World War II, after harrowing experiences in battle, or in fliers shot down during a bombing mission. The suddenness of the trauma, the lack of preparedness, would appear to have been much less pronounced in these instances, which were characterized rather by a crescendo of danger—unless we remind ourselves that the inherent narcissistic conviction of our own omnipotence results in disbelief in the ultimate trauma.

A "traumatic neurosis" can also be produced by traumatization which extends over a long period of time. In our days we have had the tragic opportunity of studying extensively thousands of these cases among survivors of concentration and

13 I am indebted to Dr. K. R. Eissler for calling my attention (in a personal communication) to the following observation made by Dr. G. Jellinek, a specialist in industrial medicine, who made a special study of accidents caused by contact with "live" wires carrying high-voltage current. The fact that *accidentally* touching such a wire frequently causes sudden death is well known. Dr. Jellinek learned to his amazement, however, that skilled electricians were often able to touch identical wires with impunity. He himself then tried touching wires carrying increasingly high-voltage current—and lived to write his book. The physiological correlates of such a preparedness for danger are not within the province of this discussion. The observation by itself, however, offers a beautiful confirmation of Freud's hypothesis concerning the importance of this preparedness in our mental economy.

[ 173 ]

extermination camps of Nazi Germany. We have also frequently seen in such cases that a single event in a long series of traumatizations stands out in memory, and remains the representative of the multitude of traumatic situations.

All these categories have in common the phenomenon emphasized by Freud: the repetitive dreams whose contents are endless variations of the traumatic situation, which includes the events preceding the actual trauma as well. Such dreams also occur in cases in which the actual trauma has been covered by a posttraumatic amnesia.

Before arriving at—or rather, expressing in so many words —the assumption that such dreams are the ultimate proof of the compulsion to repeat as the manifestation of instinctual (*triebhafte*) impulses, which in turn express "the urge to restore an earlier state of things," Freud gave a *teleological* explanation for such dreams, which would *also* deny them the property of wish fulfillment "under the dominance of the pleasure principle." He assumed that "These dreams are endeavouring to master the stimulus retrospectively, by developing the anxiety whose omission was the cause of the traumatic neurosis. They thus afford us a view of a function of the mental apparatus which, though it does not contradict the pleasure principle, is nevertheless independent of it and seems to be more primitive than the purpose of gaining pleasure and avoiding unpleasure" (p. 32).[14] At this point Freud went on to say that this was perhaps the place to "admit for the first time an exception to the proposition that dreams are fulfilments of wishes."

[14] It is puzzling that in this teleological formulation Freud on the one hand assigned to the dream the task of achieving retroactive mastery of the traumatic stimulus by developing anxiety, a task which if possible at all can be achieved only by the cathexis of certain ego structures, while on the other hand he called this function of "the dream" a "more primitive" one. This statement itself contradicts most of Freud's formulations, made at various times, about such concepts as primary process vs. secondary process, the unconscious vs. the preconscious, the id vs. the ego, and so forth.

Freud's teleological explanation of posttraumatic dreams became one of the cornerstones of his reasoning, which showed the following steps: (a) the *absence* of "fright"—that particular shade of anxiety response appropriate to the traumatic situation—along with a consequent breach of the stimulus barrier, is an important factor in the etiology of the traumatic neurosis; (b) the "aim" of posttraumatic dreams is to master the stimulus retrospectively while generating anxiety (*"unter Angstentwicklung"*); (c) the anxiety in these dreams is not a *response* to any kind of wish but something "generated" by the dreamer (we would have to say the dreamer's ego); (d) there is therefore a "beyond the pleasure principle"; (e) the aim of an "instinct" is to restore an earlier, inorganic stage; (f) such an assumption can lead only to a "death-instinct" theory; and (g) the repetition compulsion is the expression of this "instinct" toward a return to the inorganic state, and represents a regulatory principle which is not only super-ordinated to but phylogenetically and ontogenetically prior to the pleasure-unpleasure principles.

Let us reconsider at this point what I have described as the cornerstone of Freud's reasoning. Are posttraumatic dreams exceptions to Freud's proposition that dreams are fulfillments of wishes? Is anxiety not *always* a "reaction to danger" (Freud, 1926), and is the anxiety experienced in posttraumatic dreams not also a *reaction* to danger arising from a wish fulfillment, as is true of the typical "anxiety" and "punishment" dreams described by Freud? Is it not true that the ego cannot "develop," "conjure up," "create" anxiety but can only reproduce a *danger* situation within the framework of a wish fulfillment? (See Freud, 1926; for a discussion, see Schur, 1953.) If this is true for the affect anxiety, do the same considerations not also apply to the experience (affect) unpleasure?

When Freud discussed traumatic neuroses and posttraumatic dreams he was referring mainly to the manifestations of war neurosis typical of World War I, which were the topic of discussion at the Fifth International Psycho-Analytical Congress in Budapest (see Freud, 1919; Simmel, 1918). Somewhat similar clinical neurotic manifestations have been observed after peacetime accidents, although no individual psychiatrist or psychoanalyst has been able to gather information on a quantitative scale comparable to that available during the War.

World War II brought a flood of publications on war neuroses. There were more psychiatrists and psychoanalysts in the armed services than at any previous time, and the number of cases was staggering. Only a minority of such cases were strictly posttraumatic, i.e., precipitated by a single, overwhelming traumatic situation.

Extensive observations on posttraumatic neuroses were also made on survivors of the extermination camps set up by the Hitler regime. While the symptomatology of these latter neuroses lacked one symptom quite prevalent during World War I, namely, the Parkinsonlike tremor (hence the German name: *Zitterneurose,* "shaking neurosis"), all were marked by dreams in which endless variations of the traumatic situation were repeated. One of Freud's arguments in support of his interpretation of posttraumatic dreams was that patients suffering from traumatic neurosis were not "much occupied in their waking lives with memories of their accident." Freud also thought that "Perhaps they are more concerned with *not* thinking of it" (1920, p. 13).

Clinical observations do not confirm the first of these statements. It is common experience that people who have had such accidents, unless they have suffered a concussion or skull fracture with complete amnesia, talk a great deal about them and think even more about them. They are concerned about every detail of the event, but mainly with one: Why did it happen? Could it have been prevented? Whose fault

[ 176 ]

was it? In severe, psychosislike posttraumatic states observed during World War II, the traumatic event was frequently covered by an amnesia even in the absence of cerebral damage. The routine treatment was then to make the patient reconstruct the traumatic situation in a sodium pentothal interview, after which he would go through the same course of reliving, rethinking, rediscussing—and redreaming it. Survivors of Nazi extermination camps still have these dreams— more than twenty years after the events.

Freud's assumption that such patients are concerned with not thinking about the trauma implies the need for repression of the memory of it. While such a tendency may be present, this explanation is not sufficient. *What the patient really wants is the undoing of the traumatic situation,* and to this end is using a mechanism so convincingly described by Freud in his study of the Rat Man (1909c). Freud later reemphasized the special importance of undoing in the magical thinking of obsessive neurotic patients (1926, p. 120).

To return to the posttraumatic dream. Freud knew, of course, that a trauma can also represent a sexual assault, and that its repetition in dreams may represent the gratification of various id derivatives—passive, homosexual, masochistic, and others. In a footnote added in 1930 to *The Interpretation of Dreams* (1900, p. 476) Freud pointed to the importance of "punishment dreams," in which superego demands act not only in the form of "censorship," but also as motivations for the latent dream content. We also know from various accounts of traumatic neurosis in World War II that guilt over being the survivor plays an important role in its etiology and symptomatology. My own observations on survivors of extermination camps confirm the great importance of this factor.

But in another paragraph, which he added to the dream book in 1919, Freud emphasized that "punishment-dreams indicate the possibility that the ego may have a greater share

[ 177 ]

than was supposed in the construction of dreams" (p. 558). The ego's wish in the posttraumatic dreams is the continuation of the wish of the waking state: the undoing of the traumatic event. *This cannot be attempted without the re-creation of the trauma. The anxiety in such dreams is the reaction to this re-enacted trauma.* The difference between Freud's interpretation and the one suggested by me is thus the following: Freud offers two interpretations for posttraumatic dreams: (1) "These dreams are endeavouring to master the stimulus retrospectively, by developing the anxiety whose omission was the cause of the traumatic neurosis"; and (2) they are *therefore* not under the dominance of the pleasure (unpleasure) principle, but are under the dominance of the repetition compulsion, which in turn expresses the "instinct" to restore an earlier—inorganic—state of things (1920, p. 36).

According to my interpretation, the repetition of traumatic events in dreams represents—apart from the gratification of various id derivatives and superego "demands"—the ego's unconscious wish to *undo* the traumatic situation. This cannot be done without reliving the latter in endless variation. The resulting anxiety is an ego response to danger, no different from the result of other anxiety-producing dreams, in which the wish represents a forbidden instinctual (sexual or aggressive) demand.

This explanation becomes even more plausible if we think in terms of a distinction between the pleasure and unpleasure principles; in addition, it may extend at least the heuristic value of this distinction.[15] A trauma results, in terms of this distinction, not only in a "breach" of the stimulus barrier, with all the consequences described by Freud, but in a "breach" of the unpleasure principle which is meant to guarantee the avoidance of the impact of too-intensive stimula-

[15] The clinical and technical implications of my proposition will be discussed further on in this chapter.

tion of the mental apparatus, a breach which cannot be recti-
fied either by withdrawal from the source of the stimulus or
by instinctual gratification. It is the ego's function to repair
this breach. This can be done on the level of the secondary
process by reality testing, by action and thought processes
which can result in adaptation to the consequences of the
trauma, physical or psychic. It is also done on the level of the
primary process by an attempt to undo the trauma retro-
actively. We know that even such magic mechanisms may be
intertwined with the ego's attempts to regain mastery by re-
establishing reality testing. In posttraumatic dreams the
dreamer frequently becomes increasingly aware of a "dream
within a dream," of the reassuring fact that he has actually
escaped from the trauma. In other words, even the manifest
dream content may change in such a way that the traumatic
situation becomes an event of the past.[16] The analysis of such
dreams may then show how the trauma is being utilized for
the expression of various conflicts not immediately related
to it.[17]

16 In a completely different context, Stein has arrived at a similar conclusion,
namely, that the posttraumatic dream does not require an explanation "beyond the pleasure principle" (1965).

17 In his discussion of posttraumatic dreams in terms of the repetition compulsion and "beyond the pleasure principle," Freud also speculated whether
this term "beyond" could be used in a genetic, temporal sense too, stating:
"it would seem that the function of dreams, which consists in setting aside
any motives that might interrupt sleep, by fulfilling the wishes of the disturbing impulses, is not their *original* function. It would not be possible for them
to perform that function until the whole of mental life had accepted the
dominance of the pleasure principle. If there is a 'beyond the pleasure principle', it is only consistent to grant that there was also a time before the purpose of dreams was the fulfilment of wishes" (pp. 32-33).

This speculation proved to be one more example of Freud's striking fore-
sight, albeit not with regard to his hypothesis of "beyond the pleasure principle" and the repetition compulsion as expression of an inherent tendency
of instincts to restore an earlier state of things. Present-day research on dreaming has shown how early in life this phenomenon appears, so that it must use
preformed apparatuses (Hartmann, 1939) and serve certain physiological needs
*before* the maturation and differentiation of the mental apparatus can lead

This explanation of the ego aspect of posttraumatic dreams has many implications.

1. A trauma leaves the ego with an "uncompleted task" in the sense illustrated by Zeigarnik's experiments, and applied by Hartmann to the psychology of obsessive-compulsive neurosis (1933). This task the ego can handle on many levels through reality testing, adaptation, or re-establishment of ego autonomy (Hartmann, 1964). All require the ability to extend the dominance of secondary-process thinking.

In the dream—where the primary process prevails—the ego regresses to such mechanisms as undoing. Hartmann, in discussing the Zeigarnik effect, also assumes that the compulsion to repeat, which is so characteristic of the patients in that study, is based in part on their use of a magic mechanism of undoing a task left uncompleted (1933, pp. 412, 418). Hartmann's interpretation also takes cognizance of Freud's previously quoted statement about the role of the ego in the construction of dreams.

2. My explanation is nothing more than an application of Freud's remark concerning the ego's involvement in the dream work. For obvious reasons our attention has been directed primarily toward the defensive function of the ego in the dream. However, Hartmann (1939, 1948, 1964) has been emphasizing the importance of both the pleasure derived from functioning (see also Groos's [1901] and Bühler's *Funktionslust* [1930]) and the pleasure derived from the effect of an activity.[18] Hartmann has stated repeatedly that ego interests, and the "pleasure" derived from ego activities and

---

to structure development (Fisher, 1965). At that early stage we cannot yet speak of wish fulfillment or the pleasure-unpleasure principles as psychological concepts (see Schur, 1964).

18 White's "efficacy concept" (1963), which for him is a central point in a system that he uses to dispute many basic formulations of the psychoanalytic theory of affects (anxiety) and of Hartmann's concept of neutralization, seems to be only an elaboration of these concepts. See also Jahoda (1966).

[ 180 ]

their results, cannot be explained *only* by instinctual drive gratification, although the latter plays an important role in producing this "pleasure." The concept "wish" as formulated by Freud with reference to instinctual gratification (1900, pp. 565, 598) thus also applies to gratification of ego demands, whether these be reality oriented or not. Kurt Lewin's "quasi-needs" (1935) can therefore, as Hartmann has postulated (1933, p. 418), also be seen in metapsychological terms as applying to the demands (needs, wishes) of the ego. The logical conclusion, therefore, is that the pleasure and unpleasure principles also apply to such ego wishes. Hence we may further conclude that the development of the reality principle is influenced not only by frustrations of instinctual demands, but by frustrations of ego demands as well, under the influences of the unpleasure principle. The need for the gratification of instinctual demands which cannot be supplied by the environment in response to simple signals, the need for delay or for alloplastic action, and also the frustration of ego needs and gratifications may stimulate learning, and therefore also the establishment of the reality principle, if such frustrations are not traumatic.[19] The frustration of instinctual needs stimulates the discovery of new avenues of gratification; uncompleted ego tasks stimulate inventiveness.

3. If, in accordance with my objections, Freud's interpretation of the posttraumatic dream as beyond the pleasure principle is not valid, then it can no longer remain the "cornerstone" of Freud's hypotheses of (a) the repetition compulsion as a superordinated regulating principle beyond the pleasure principle; (b) instinct as an "urge inherent in organic life to restore an earlier state of things" (i.e., the inorganic state); and, finally, (c) the death-instinct concept. However, all this does not negate the fact that repetitiveness as

19 Frustrations can be traumatic by their sheer quantity or duration, or because of the developmental phase in which they occur.

such is a ubiquitous biological phenomenon, and that alternation between organic life and inorganic states may be a phenomenon applying to the entire cosmos. But such considerations are beyond the framework of psychology.[20]

4. Once we have accepted the interpretation that post-traumatic dreams *can* be understood without recourse to the existence of a "daemonic force" (1920, p. 35)—conceptualized in terms of the repetition compulsion—by the application of the pleasure and unpleasure principles to both *id and ego* aspects of such dreams, it becomes easier to explain along similar lines the other examples cited by Freud in support of his hypothesis:

It is true that the neurotic endlessly repeats the manifestations of his "transference neurosis" inside the psychoanalytic situation (Stone, 1961), while outside that situation he repeatedly "acts out" painful, often traumatic situations which cannot bring him any "pleasure" in the experiential sense of the word. Freud tried to use these phenomena to support his hypothesis concerning the existence of a daemonic force, a repetition compulsion beyond the pleasure principle, and a death instinct.[21] Here again, as in his discussion of anxiety dreams, Freud acknowledged that some unpleasurable experiences of this kind occur in the analytic situation because that

20 I have elsewhere (1966) tried to elucidate the factors which may have contributed to Freud's death-instinct theory. I found a clue to these in the following paragraph of *Beyond the Pleasure Principle*: "Perhaps we have adopted the belief because there is some comfort in it. If we are to die ourselves, and first to lose in death those who are dearest to us, it is easier to submit to a remorseless law of nature, to the sublime *Ananke* [Necessity], than to a chance which might perhaps have been escaped. It may be, however, that this belief in the internal necessity of dying is only another of those illusions which we have created '*um die Schwere des Daseins zu ertragen*' " (p. 45) .

21 Many authors, who have discussed the repetition compulsion but who do not subscribe to the death-instinct theory, have skirted the fact that Freud's view of the repetition compulsion as a superordinated regulatory principle is inseparable from his death-instinct theory (Bibring, 1936; Waelder, 1932; Lipin, 1963). See also Gifford (1964). For a more detailed bibliography on the repetition compulsion, see Schur (1960a).

situation encourages the reliving of the past, the submission of past wishes and fears to reality testing, and the replacement of psychic reality by reality proper. He acknowledged that some of the unpleasure experienced by the ego can be explained within the framework of the pleasure (unpleasure) principles: "unpleasure for one system and simultaneously satisfaction for the other" (1920, p. 20; see also 1900, pp. 580-581). However, he went on to say: "But we come now to a new and remarkable fact, namely that the compulsion to repeat also recalls from the past experiences which include no possibility of pleasure, and which can never, even long ago, have brought satisfaction even to instinctual impulses which have since been repressed." Which examples did Freud then cite of such "past experiences"? They include most of the unsatisfied sexual fantasies and strivings of the oedipal and preoedipal periods, the various narcissistic injuries, the aggressive impulses of the oedipal situation and of sibling rivalry, all of which are repeated in the transference situation. But can we not say that *most* sexual, aggressive, and omnipotent fantasies, even of later life, *never* meet with satisfaction? This certainly applies to most of the wishes which represent instinctual danger, elicit signal anxiety, and are subject to repression or other defenses. Such wishes, which are completely distorted in dreams, frequently result in anxiety and can be detected in symptom formation. How can we explain the distinction made by Freud in the two sentences quoted above? Only by recognizing that Freud, in his second formulation—the one that makes it possible for him to support his hypothesis of the repetition compulsion as a superordinated principle—uses the terms "pleasure" and "satisfaction" in their experiential sense. In this context "pleasure" and "satisfaction" are presented as affects within the framework of structural formulations. The concepts pleasure and unpleasure *principles* as regulatory principles, or rather tendencies, were formulated by Freud in economic terms. The pleasure principle implies the tendency toward drive discharge for purposes of eliminating tension. The unpleasure principle implies the tendency to avoid increased tension from internal or external sources. Freud's concepts of wish (1900) and instinctual drives having an "aim" and an "object" (1915a) are formulated within this same economic framework (see Chapter 4). Developmentally, the experience of pleasure appears later, of course, than tension reduction through need-drive satisfaction.

As mentioned before, the gratification of all instinctual wishes (fantasies, drive derivatives) is impossible for biological reasons in the widest sense of the word. Defenses, the development of the reality principle and of the superego therefore have eminent survival value for the phenotype and genotype of *Homo sapiens*.

That infantile sexuality and aggression in most of their aspects are doomed to frustration is a fact which Freud himself repeatedly stressed.

We can assume only that Freud's conclusions, drawn from the fact that certain drive derivatives and the behavior motivated by them result in unpleasure, are an example of *ad hoc* reasoning used to prove a preformed hypothesis—namely, that such behavior is motivated by a repetition compulsion, a manifestation of the death instinct. This way of thinking, which is so different from Freud's general scientific style, can be detected throughout *Beyond the Pleasure Principle*.

I agree with the many authors (e.g., Greenacre, 1963, 1964; Lipin, 1963; Stein, 1965; Brodsky, 1964, to mention only a few) who emphasize the importance of early traumatic experiences, and point out that early traumatization manifests itself in the analytic situation by an intense compulsion to repeat, which represents a formidable obstacle to working through. Early, intense, usually protracted traumatization interferes with the integration of primitive, pregenital drives into the genital organization, and with the development of ego functions essential for the establishment of the reality principle, frustration tolerance, secondary ego autonomy (Hartmann, 1939, 1950, 1964), the neutralization of aggression (Hartmann, 1950, 1964; Hartmann, Kris, and Loewenstein, 1949), and, principally, the achievement of object constancy (Hartmann, 1952, 1964; Jacobson, 1964; Mahler, 1963). Traumatic experiences also interfere with normal development because they acquire the valence of an organizing factor. The traumatic events with all their consequences attract an inordinate quantity of countercathexis, which must result in a restriction of ego autonomy. It is obvious that such cases demonstrate both in the analytic situation and in acting-out episodes a compulsion to repeat accompanied by a great deal of unpleasure. But such phenomena prove only that the discharge of primitive libidinal and aggressive drives must either be inhibited or result primarily in unpleasure; they do not prove Freud's hypothesis of a repetition compulsion based on the death instinct; they therefore do not necessarily preclude successful analysis.

Before discussing the pertinence of Freud's last argument in support of his hypothesis—the play of children—I believe it would be useful to consider some of the clinical and technical implications of my discussion of Freud's hypotheses, in view of the well-founded maxim that any theoretical reformulation may and should be applicable to clinical observation.

Freud's concepts of the repetition compulsion, the death instinct, and instinct as an urge to re-create an earlier (inorganic) state were characterized by him as "far-fetched speculations." We know that Freud, the pragmatist, utilized theoretical hypotheses for clinical formulations. We can trace the hypotheses under discussion along two different paths. Of these, one proved to be heuristically extremely meaningful, namely, the importance of the aggressive instinctual drive. This concept could be utilized and developed *without* recourse to the concepts repetition compulsion and death instinct. Whenever Freud resorted to formulations utilizing the concepts death instinct and repetition compulsion as a superordinated regulatory principle, "beyond the pleasure principle"—as he did, for example, in *Civilization and Its Discontents* or the *Outline*—these remained simply controversial hypotheses. But when Freud and others (most recently Lipin, for example) use these concepts for clinical, technical purposes, especially in connection with such problems as working through, it is evident that the question of the validity of these concepts gains in importance.

In "Analysis Terminable and Interminable" (1937), his last major work dealing with the technique of psychoanalysis, Freud, after discussing the resistances of certain groups of patients who showed utter rigidity in their defenses and whose mental processes were immutable, made the statement:

> Here we are dealing with the ultimate things which psychological research can learn about: the behaviour of the two primal instincts, their distribution, mingling[22] and defusion—things which we cannot think of as being confined to a single province of the mental apparatus, the id, the ego, or the super-ego. No stronger impression arises from the resistances during the work of analysis than of there being a force which is defending itself by every possible means against recovery and which is absolutely resolved to hold on to illness and suffering. One portion of this force has been recognized by us, undoubtedly with justice, as the sense of guilt and need for punishment, and has been localized by us in the ego's relation to the superego . . . other quotas of the same force . . . may be at work in other, unspecified places. . . . These phenomena are un-

[22] Joan Riviere's translation (see *Collected Papers,* Vol. V, p. 345) of this word as "fusion" seems to be more accurate than "mingling."

mistakable indications of the presence of a power in mental life which we call the instinct of aggression or of destruction according to its aims, and which we trace back to the original death instinct of living matter [pp. 242-243].

Here the repetition compulsion and the death instinct are used as explanatory concepts with regard to the immutability of certain patients in analysis.[23] This application of theory has had many undesirable consequences: it has given us an easy out for the lack of success in certain cases, and must, if taken seriously, create a greater-than-healthy skepticism. Assigning to this type of defense the term "id resistance" and locating its source in the death instinct must create a fatalistic attitude in the analyst.

Greenson, in his paper on working through (1965), discussed this point tangentially; one of his cases presented typical immutability and "adhesiveness" of the libido described by Freud as characteristic for the dominance of the repetition compulsion. The working through of a peculiar hierarchical intertwining of defenses resulted in a successful solution of the conflicts in this case.

Greenacre (1964) has rightly emphasized the necessity of tracing back *all* elements of faulty development to ascertain what disruption was related to various traumatic events (see also Brodsky, 1964).[24]

23 Freud did not have in mind psychotic patients, for whom he considered analysis to be impossible for other reasons.

24 Lipin (1963), in a thoughtful and imaginative paper, tried to explain certain behavioral phenomena manifested by patients in the analytic situation, which Freud had described in *Beyond the Pleasure Principle* and "Analysis Terminable and Interminable." Taking as his point of departure Freud's concept of the repetition compulsion as "beyond the pleasure principle," Lipin offered a complex genetic hypothesis differentiating between "maturational" and "instinctual" drive representations. According to this hypothesis, what are described as "maturational" drive representations are genetically older, more primitive, "beyond the pleasure principle," and subject to regulation by the repetition compulsion as Freud used the term. Lipin thus avoided bringing into his own genetic formulations any consideration of the inseparable rela-

I have assumed that the magic wish to *undo* a trauma plays an important part in the formation of posttraumatic dreams. I would assume that the same mechanism also plays an important part in many instances of impervious resistance to working through. While this is not the place for a comprehensive discussion or the presentation of pertinent case material, I want to mention certain types of patients who demonstrate this kind of resistance. In their cases we can utilize the analysis of this resistance to aid in the process of working through.

1. One example has actually already been discussed, both by Freud and many others, but not within the framework of the mechanism of undoing; this is the frequent experience of women in the last phases of their analyses who go through a period of depression when they are forced to realize that analysis will not equip them with a penis. It is not only the futile wish to acquire a penis which must be renounced, but also the wish to undo the very fact of their different equipment, and the conviction that the latter depended on the volition of their parents.

2. A second, equally well-known example occurs in the analysis of women who must realize, too late, that the right time has passed for finding a proper mate and bearing children. Here, too, the ultimate resistance expresses itself not only in intolerance for this frustration, but in a wish that the clock be turned back and their whole past be undone. It is impossible for them to accept Shakespeare's dictum: "What's done is done, and can't be undone" (*Macbeth*).

3. Less transparent is the functioning of this mechanism in cases where early, severe traumatization has occurred, and the main symptom is one of masochistic character disorder

---

tionship in Freud's conceptualization among the repetition compulsion, the general nature of instinct as an urge to restore an earlier, inorganic state, and the death instinct, of which the repetition compulsion is a manifestation.

with a tendency to depression. In these patients the compulsion to repeat is seemingly endless, both in and outside the analytic hour. Reconstruction and recall result in little, or painfully slow, change. They expect the change to come from the analyst or some other figure in the environment. What impresses one as clinging dependency and occasionally sulky accusations with paranoid undertones can be revealed as a projection of the same magic wish to undo the past: severe childhood illness, accidents and surgery, tragedies caused by war, real or highly hypothetical genetic defects, parents who either could not counteract these traumatizations or were actually responsible for them.

4. The last example applies to those patients who come to realize in the course of their analyses in how many ways their intellectual development has been threatened by the combination of early traumatization and deprivation through a primitive, nonstimulating environment.

All the above-mentioned attempts at undoing are doomed to failure. It is too early to say definitely how much the recognition and analysis of this type of resistance can contribute to the overcoming of obstacles to working through. It is obvious that the age of the patient plays an important role.

To turn now to the last of Freud's examples offered in substantiation of his hypotheses—certain types of children's play. In his initial discussion of his observations (1920, pp. 14-17), Freud introduced the brilliant interpretation that the child was repeating actively what he had undergone passively. Innumerable examples of this have since been added by observers of child behavior.

At this time Freud acknowledged that all the phenomena of children's play described by him still gave "no evidence of . . . tendencies *beyond* the pleasure principle" (p. 17). That Freud was of two minds about characterizing the type of children's play that re-created unpleasurable experiences as an expression of the repetition compulsion can be seen from a later statement in which he actually contradicted the preceding quotation: "Now too we shall be inclined to relate to this [repetition] compulsion the dreams which occur in traumatic neuroses and the impulse which leads children to play" (pp. 22-23). However, some pages later he stated:

> The manifestations of a compulsion to repeat (which we have described as occurring in the early activities of infantile mental life as well as among the events of psychoanalytic treatment) exhibit to a high degree an instinctual[25] character and, when they act in opposition to the pleasure principle, give the appearance of some 'daemonic' force at work. In the case of children's play we seemed to see that children repeat unpleasurable experiences for the additional reason that they can master a powerful impression far more thoroughly by being active than they could by merely experiencing it passively. . . . Nor can children have their *pleasurable* experiences repeated often enough. . . . This character trait disappears later on. . . . Novelty is always the condition of enjoyment. But children will never tire of asking an adult to repeat a game that he has shown them or played with them till he is too exhausted to go on. . . . None of this contradicts the pleasure principle; repetition, the re-experiencing of something identical, is clearly in itself a source of pleasure. In the case of a person in analysis, on the contrary, the compulsion to repeat the events of his childhood in the transference evidently disregards the pleasure principle in every way [pp. 35-36].

Having characterized this compulsion to repeat as "instinctual," Freud then introduced his definition of an instinct as an urge to restore an earlier, inorganic state (p. 36).

---

[25] *Triebhaft*, in German. In this context "instinctive" (as pertaining to the biological concept instinct) would be a more appropriate translation.

In these paragraphs, so packed with brilliant observations and deductions, Freud drew a distinction between the repetitiveness of play and the "daemonic" repetition compulsion manifesting itself, according to him, in the transference situation. The fact that Freud alternated between extending the concept of the "daemonic" aspect of the repetition compulsion to the play of children and explaining the latter on different grounds illuminates both the difficulty and the necessity of distinguishing between repetitiveness, a compulsion to repeat, and a superordinated regulating principle based on the death instinct.

It is therefore remarkable that the concept of repetition compulsion was unhesitatingly applied to the activities of children by Waelder (1932) and Nunberg (1937), although Waelder, in contrast to Nunberg, does not subscribe to the death-instinct theory. I have indicated at some length—and I hope convincingly—that Freud's concept of the repetition compulsion is inseparable from his general hypothesis of instinct as an urge to restore an earlier state of things, and more specifically, from his death-instinct theory.

We might abandon the term repetition compulsion altogether and substitute another to refer to the types of psychic manifestation described by Freud under this heading. The logical alternative—"compulsion to repeat"—has to some extent been pre-empted by Strachey's translation of Freud's term *"Wiederholungszwang"* ("repetition compulsion") in this manner throughout the *Standard Edition*. Other alternatives might be "compulsive repetitiveness" or "compulsive stereotyped repetitiveness." Any author wishing to continue to use "repetition compulsion" would be obliged, at least for some time, to indicate that he was not denoting a behavior pattern motivated by the death instinct. Spitz (1937) and Peller (1954, 1955) extensively discussed the repetitive aspect of play, especially up to the age of six, *without* referring to the repetition-compulsion concept.[26]

I have tried to show in my discussion that none of Freud's psychological adductions used to substantiate his hypothesis of "beyond the pleasure principle" and the concepts of the

26 How impossible it is to accept the concept repetition compulsion within the framework of Freud's hypothesis is shown by Bibring's discussion (1943). Without repudiating Freud's hypothesis in so many words, so sharp a thinker as Bibring arrives at such formulations as: "The repetition compulsion is the expression of the 'inertia' of living matter, of the conservative trend to maintain and repeat intensive experiences" (p. 487). Bibring fails to point out, however, that Freud used the term "inertia" to express the urge of all organic matter to return to an earlier, inorganic state.

Further on Bibring arrives at a complete impasse in attempting to correlate Freud's hypotheses of the repetition compulsion with the "death" and "life" instincts, when he says: "Thus what Freud called death instincts would become life instincts, because they would repeat the trauma of the formation of life, and vice versa the life instincts would become death instincts, because they had to repeat the painful trauma of dispersing living matter" (pp. 488-489). Bibring then abandons the attempt to reconcile the repetition compulsion with Freud's death-instinct theory, while still accepting Freud's assumption that the repetition compulsion is beyond the pleasure principle. As he says in a highly cryptic statement: "It aims at explaining certain 'compulsive' repetitions by the assumed tendency of the instincts to surrender to the formative influence of overwhelmingly intense, powerful, 'traumatic' impressions, whether pleasurable or painful" (p. 514). Other statements describe the dilemma: "The repetition compulsion is beyond the pleasure principle but not absolutely opposed to it. It exists, as it were, prior to the pleasure principle and is broader, since it can fix both the pleasurable and the painful. It exerts a certain influence on the pleasure principle by fixing the instincts aiming at pleasure to certain objects and aims" (p. 508). "The given examples provide an opportunity of confirming that the repetition compulsion can enter into union either with the narcissistic pleasure of the ego (*Ichlust*) or with the instinctual satisfaction (*Eslust*)" (p. 509).

It is also significant that, for Bibring, the application of the concept repetition compulsion to the traumatic neuroses—which to Freud represented the cornerstone of his hypothesis—remains most doubtful. The explanation lies in the fact that Bibring is preoccupied with such formulations as the "counter-cathectic" aspect of the ego "against the trauma" and against anxiety and the aspect of "abreaction of the tension in small doses."

Nothing expresses Bibring's difficulty better than his conclusion in which he also takes into account Hendrick's (1942) discussion of the repetition compulsion. Bibring says: "Generally speaking, there are three possibilities of placing the repetition compulsion. One may refer it to the instinctual drives of the id, or to the ego instincts, or to both. This leads to three different conceptions of the repetition compulsion. If we ascribe it only to the id, it would

repetition compulsion and the death instinct are valid; that all the examples cited by Freud—certain types of children's play; the reproduction of unpleasurable experiences in the analytic situation and in acting out; and, above all, traumatic dreams—can be explained within the framework of the pleasure and unpleasure principles, especially when we differentiate between these two and apply them both to the functioning of the ego. With regard to Freud's examples drawn from animal behavior—such as the migration of birds and fish—both the exponents of the term "instinct" such as ethologists (e.g., Lorenz, 1937; Tinbergen, 1951) who emphasize the innate character of instinctive behavior and "biopsychologists" (e.g., Schneirla, 1956) agree that all phenomena of this kind are based on certain species-specific response patterns to very specific perceptual stimuli and not on a tendency to repeat an earlier phase of their existence.

To subsume the phenomena of genetic transmission, which is of course the substrate of embryological development as well, under the concept of "instinct" is even more far-fetched.[27]

---

unavoidably be conceived as an instinctual automatism, as tension repetition or as fixation repetition. If we refer it to the ego only, it necessarily is comprehended as restitutive or regulative dynamism. If one attributes the repetition compulsion simultaneously to both the id drives and the ego instincts then probably one would accept Hendrick's conclusions" (p. 517). Here Bibring returns to a division of the instincts into id and ego instincts, a division repudiated by Freud when he introduced his new dual-instinct theory (1920).

I have discussed Bibring's paper rather extensively because it is still considered to be a basic contribution to this problem. As stated at the beginning of this chapter, I cannot engage in a thorough discussion of the whole literature on this topic.

[27] Freud's excursions into biology to prove the existence not only of Thanatos but of Eros are equally speculative. When he finally could not withstand the temptation to invoke Plato's *Symposium* and the *Upanishads*, he stated disarmingly: "In quite a different region [from science] . . . we *do* meet with such a hypothesis [about the origin of sexuality]; but it is of so fantastic a kind—a myth rather than a scientific explanation—that I should not venture to produce it here, were it not that it fulfils precisely the one condition whose fulfilment we desire. For it traces the origin of an instinct to *a need to restore an earlier state of things*" (p. 57).

# 16

## *Repetitiveness as an Adaptive and Regressive Phenomenon*

Nᴏɴᴇ ᴏꜰ ᴍʏ discussion is meant to detract from (a) the importance of repetitiveness for the maturation and development of structures and hence for adaptation and learning; (b) the importance of repetitiveness in abnormal behavior, and especially in the transference phenomenon and acting out in the psychoanalytic situation.

The genetic, structural, and adaptive problems of repetitiveness and automatization have been discussed extensively by Hartmann (1939; see also Bibring, 1943). He, too, tried to delineate the adaptive aspects of these phenomena and their importance for learning, and distinguished them from the concept of repetition compulsion as used by Freud, as well as by Nunberg (1932, 1937) and Waelder (1932).

Hartmann (1939) applies the term "automatism" only "to the somatic and preconscious ego apparatuses" (p. 90), and states in a most meaningful sentence that "Automatization is a characteristic example of those relatively stable forms of adaptedness which are the lasting effects of adaptation processes" (p. 92). He rightly stresses the essential difference between normal, adaptive automatisms and "ego rigidity" or "pathological automatisms." He also rightly stresses that automatisms persist in an adaptive way throughout life: "the normal ego must be *able* to control, but it must also be *able to must"* (p. 94). In a discussion at a meeting of the New York Psychoanalytic Society Hartmann is quoted by Bibring to have summarized his views on repetitiveness as follows:

> . . . repetition occurs: '(1) in response to the same stimuli; (2) when what was experienced resulted in pleasure (or in the avoidance of pain) or was pleasurable in itself (repetitions in childhood, especially of newly learned activities, belong to this category); (3) in connection with automatisms of thoughts and actions. This leads to the reaching of the same or very similar solutions of certain problems. In this case a kind of independence of the pleasure principle —at least to a certain degree—seems to be evident. Such automatisms multiply in the course of life, whereas the typical repetitions of the child decrease in the latency period (Spitz). (4) Repetition also occurs when intended actions were not completed and have therefore the tendency to repetition, as actions or thoughts. This can be proved experimentally (K. Lewin). (5) Repetition occurs when traumatic experiences have not been assimilated' [Bibring, 1943, p. 491].

Freud's examples of repetitiveness, with the exception of the play of children, where he himself was not quite convinced of the applicability of the repetition-compulsion concept, were taken from pathological conditions (traumatic neurosis, transference neurosis, fate neurosis). From these Freud then extrapolated the repetition compulsion as a ubiquitous phenomenon characteristic of "instincts." Only the last point of Hartmann's summary deals with such pathological conditions. I have proposed the term "compulsive (stereotyped) repetitiveness," characteristic of all the examples given by Freud, to replace "repetition compulsion." We have learned from Freud that pathology can be understood only by a genetic study of normal development. Repetitiveness is characteristic not only of the play of children (Spitz, 1937; Peller, 1954) but of *all* behavior of infants and prelatency children. We can go even further and say that repetitiveness is characteristic of animal behavior. We can establish a direct relationship between a relative lack of autonomy from drives (physiological needs on the "biophysiological" level of evolution and development) and environmental stimuli, and more or less stereotyped repetitiveness of behavior. The human infant can use certain apparatuses of primary autonomy, but is otherwise prey to stimulation from the inner and outer environment. Frustration *and* gratification, coupled with the maturation of all apparatuses, lead in a spiraling path to the acquisition (assimilation, in Piaget's term) of new skills. The repertoire of repetitive actions grows, without initially affecting the character of repetitiveness. What Spitz (1937) has described with regard to the play of children, namely, a gradual shift away from more or less rigid repetitiveness to an ability to choose variations, applies also to other activities. The occupation of each new way station, however, requires a certain consolidation through repetitiveness.

It is for this reason that Hartmann (although he refrains from a discussion of all the implications of the concept repetition compulsion) emphasizes, rightly, that "we must not take every repetition for an expression of the repetition compulsion" (1939, p. 96).

Only when we look upon the repetition compulsion as a "daemonic" superordinated force can we speak, with Nunberg, of "the constant struggle between the retarding tendencies of the repetition-compulsion and the hunger for new impressions that leads little by little to the mastering of reality. In the course of this process the repetition-compulsion gradually recedes into the background" (1937, p. 171). With increasing secondary autonomy, the ego gains increased margins of choice. While it is true that rigid repetitiveness (immutability) has been viewed as characteristic of the instinctual drives and of behavior motivated by them, I have just pointed out that repetitiveness is also characteristic of behavior responses to external stimulation. Repetitiveness is thus inherent in all physiological and psychological structures. The more a behavior pattern is under the influence of autonomous ego structures, the more flexible and reality-oriented it will be. This may also mean that a given reality will require freely choosing "to must" or to relinquish autonomy "in the service of the ego" (Kris, 1934).

Not only in the transference and fate neuroses, but in every severe neurosis, behavior is the result of unconscious primitive id derivatives, such as pregenital wishes and fantasies and poorly neutralized aggressive strivings, along with rigid, often primitive, defense structures. This combination results in a tendency toward compulsive, stereotyped repetitiveness.

Such behavior patterns are regressive, not only because they result from the regression of drives to early points of fixation, and the regression of various ego functions, but also because the resulting repetitive behavior pattern corresponds to a more primitive, infantile level.[1] The concepts of a continuum and of a complementary series also apply, of course, to the degree of such regressions. In this sense Freud's contention that the repetitiveness represents a return to a previous state is correct. However, the "previous" state in question is not an inorganic one but an infantile one. We might add that such regression leads to man's "being lived" rather than "living," which is the case with certain lower forms of animals (Schur, 1958).

To discuss the reality principle in this monograph would be largely to repeat what Hartmann (1956a) has already cov-

---

[1] I have stated in a previous publication (1960a) that stereotyped compulsive behavior, where the ego's executive apparatuses are still, or have again become, completely dependent on ("passive" in relation to) the instinctual drives and external stimulation, is reminiscent of "instinctive" behavior patterns, which are phylogenetically and ontogenetically older than learned behavior patterns.

[ 197 ]

ered. I would only reiterate the points made earlier (Chapter 11) that both the pleasure principle, which regulates the need to achieve gratification, and the unpleasure principle, which regulates the necessity to avoid unpleasure, contribute to structure formation (learning) and thereby also to the creation of such ego structures as will guarantee the establishment of the reality principle (Schur, 1962).

In discussing the ego mechanism of undoing in connection with posttraumatic dreams and the transference neurosis, I pointed out that even this magical defense mechanism, which, in conjunction with the constant demands of primitive instinctual strivings, results in compulsive repetitive behavior, can, under certain conditions, result in the mastery of traumatic experience or conflict.[2]

---

[2] This is in line with Hartmann's statement that the repetition compulsion (especially in what he calls its "domesticated" form) may have its share in the learning processes (1939, p. 98).

# 17

## Summary and Conclusions

I BEGAN this monograph with the purpose of clarifying and, if possible, eliminating certain ambiguities in the concept id. This required a detailed discussion of the development of this concept, as well as others which are intrinsic to it, such as the instinctual drives, the primary process, the pleasure-unpleasure principles, and so forth. It soon became apparent that the latter two concepts, particularly the second, transcended the original topic and required a semi-independent discussion. This monograph, therefore, consists of two parts.

The genetic point of view and the concept of a continuum have been the cornerstone of my considerations about the id. When I postulate that the id *and* the instinctual drives are both phylogenetically and ontogenetically the product of evolution, maturation, and development, I am merely drawing logical conclusions from the many formulations of Freud, extensively quoted by me. I am also drawing the necessary conclusions from the concept of an undifferentiated phase (Hartmann, 1950; Hartmann and Kris, 1945; Hartmann, Kris, and Loewenstein, 1946). I also find myself in agreement with Gill (1963), Rapaport (1960b), and Kestenberg (1953), among others.

*I assume that certain autonomous apparatuses serve the development not only of the ego but of the id as well.* This also applies to the apparatuses serving the functions of perception and memory. The concept "wish" and its development are to be understood in such terms. Freud's statement that "the id . . . has a world of perception of its own" (1940, p. 198) gains another perspective in this light. We need only paraphrase it by saying that the id makes use of certain percepts which either arise from within the organism or are perceived as such, even if they originate from without; that these are transformed in primary-process terms and are subject to "regulation" by the pleasure-unpleasure principles. These genetic considerations must assign to the id some content and adaptive function.[1] I assume that these formulations are also in line with those which Freud expressed in various terms concerning the working of this structure of the mental apparatus, which "remains the most important throughout life" (1940, p. 145, n. 2), about the "processes which are possible in and between the assumed psychical elements in the id (the *primary process*)" (1940, p. 198).

The concept of a continuum is essential to our understanding of all psychic phenomena. That there are no strict delineations between id and ego is part and parcel of this concept, as well as the fact that there are no strict delineations between physiological needs and their mental representations conceptualized as drives and wishes. The structural point of view would become much less meaningful if divorced from the genetic and dynamic points of view. The dynamic point of view, which has been so essential for the development of psychoanalysis and for our understanding of the fact that conflicts and the attempts to resolve them are crucial for normal and abnormal development, would also become meaningless if we tried to consider structures only from an economic point of view.

While in man the ego is the main "organ of adaptation" and guarantees survival, adaptation must mediate among in-

[1] I thus arrive from genetic considerations at formulations similar to those of Gill in his monograph.

[ 200 ]

stinctual wishes, ego and superego demands, and the environment. The instinctual demands, which we "assign" to the id, are therefore also essential both to adaptation and survival. These formulations are not meant to detract from the importance of economic formulations, which are meaningful and heuristically valid concepts, but are meant only to discourage the assumption that an economic formulation can be sufficiently meaningful per se without a consideration of the other metapsychological points of view.

In Chapter 11 on "The Regulatory Principles of Mental Functioning," I have tried to reconsider and to clarify the meaning of these "principles." The following conclusions seem to me to be warranted:

1. A distinction between the pleasure and unpleasure principles should be made on evolutional and developmental grounds. Such a distinction can also be traced to Freud's own formulations, and seems to be heuristically fruitful from both the theoretical and clinical points of view.

2. A strict delineation between the pleasure and unpleasure principles as *regulatory principles,* and the *affective experiences* of pleasure and unpleasure, is essential to our understanding.

3. A detailed discussion of Freud's *Beyond the Pleasure Principle,* undertaken in an attempt to elucidate the repetition-compulsion concept, led to the following points:

a. I am convinced that Freud's concept of the repetition compulsion is inseparable from the following hypotheses: the repetition compulsion operates beyond the pleasure principle; the repetition compulsion is an expression of "instinctual" (or rather "instinctive") behavior; an "instinct" is an urge inherent in organic life to restore an earlier (inorganic) state of things; this, then, presupposes a death instinct; the repetition compulsion thus becomes a manifestation of the death instinct. It is therefore a contradiction in terms

[ 201 ]

for an author to use Freud's concept of the repetition compulsion as *beyond* the pleasure principle *without* subscribing to the definition of instinct, specifically of the death instinct, given in *Beyond the Pleasure Principle*. What such an author actually has in mind, when speaking of the repetition compulsion in conjunction with "beyond the pleasure principle," is the *experiential* aspect of pleasure and unpleasure, and not the regulatory pleasure and unpleasure *principles*.

b. I have tried to show that none of Freud's examples (primarily posttraumatic dreams, the transference and fate neuroses, the play of children) validate his hypotheses; that all these examples can be explained within the framework of the pleasure and unpleasure principles, as long as we distinguish between a regulatory principle and an affective experience, and bear in mind the well-known patterns of behavior which are mainly under the influence of the instinctual demands, the regressive aspect of compulsive stereotyped repetitiveness, and certain magical ego defense mechanisms of undoing. I have discussed the theoretical and technical implications of the recognition of such ego defenses, and have therefore transcended in this chapter the limits of the concept id.

c. For all the aforementioned reasons, I have suggested substituting the term "compulsive (stereotyped) repetitiveness" for the term "repetition compulsion."

d. I have refrained from discussing the reality principle, in view of Hartmann's exhaustive treatment of this topic, and have restricted myself to a few remarks concerning the influence of both the pleasure and unpleasure principles on learning, and thereby on the establishment of the reality principle.

# Bibliography

ANDERSSON, O. (1962), *Studies in the Prehistory of Psychoanalysis*. Uppsala: Scandinavian University Books.

ARLOW, J. A. (1958), Report on Panel: The Psychoanalytic Theory of Thinking. *J. Amer. Psychoanal. Assn.*, 6:143-153.

—— (1963), Conflict, Regression, and Symptom Formation. *Int. J. Psycho-Anal.*, 44:12-22.

—— & BRENNER, C. (1964), *Psychoanalytic Concepts and the Structural Theory [Journal of the American Psychoanalytic Association Monograph Series, No. 3]*. New York: International Universities Press.

BENJAMIN, J. D. (1961), The Innate and the Experiential. In: *Lectures in Experimental Psychiatry*, ed. H. W. Brosin. Pittsburgh: University of Pittsburgh Press, pp. 19-42.

BERES, D. (1962), Contribution to Panel: The Concept of the Id, rep. E. Marcovitz. *J. Amer. Psychoanal. Assn.*, 11:151-160, 1963.

—— (1965), Structure and Function in Psychoanalysis. Read at the New York Psychoanalytic Society, January 12. Abst. in *Psychoanal. Quart.*, 34:629-631.

BIBRING, E. (1936), The Development and Problems of the Theory of the Instincts. *Int. J. Psycho-Anal.*, 22:102-131, 1941.

—— (1943), The Conception of the Repetition Compulsion. *Psychoanal. Quart.*, 12:486-519.

BRENNER, C. (1955), *An Elementary Textbook of Psychoanalysis*. New York: International Universities Press.

BREUER, J. & FREUD, S. (1893-1895), Studies on Hysteria. *Standard Edition*, 2. London: Hogarth Press, 1955.

BRODSKY, B. H. (1964), Two Contributions to the Theory of Working Through. Read at the New York Psychoanalytic Society, October 13. Abst. in *Psychoanal. Quart.*, 34:319-321.

BRUNSWICK, D. (1954), A Revision of the Classification of Instincts or Drives. *Int. J. Psycho-Anal.*, 35:224-228.

BÜHLER, K. (1930), *Kindheit und Jugend*. Leipzig: Hirzel.

EIDELBERG, L. (1962), A Contribution to the Study of the Unpleasure-Pleasure Principle. *Psychiat. Quart.*, 36:312-316.

EISSLER, K. R. (1962), On the Metapsychology of the Preconscious: A Tentative Contribution to Psychoanalytic Morphology. *The Psychoanalytic Study of the Child*, 17:9-41. New York: International Universities Press.

FENICHEL, O. (1945), *The Psychoanalytic Theory of Neurosis*. New York: Norton.

FISHER, C. (1954), Dreams and Perception: The Role of Preconscious and Primary Modes of Perception in Dream Formation. *J. Amer. Psychoanal. Assn.*, 2:389-445.

—— (1957), A Study of the Preliminary Stages of the Construction of Dreams and Images. *J. Amer. Psychoanal. Assn.*, 5:5-60.

—— (1961), Discussion of: The Structuring of Drive and Reality: David Rapaport's Contribution to the Science of Psychology, by M. M. Gill & G. S. Klein. Read at the New York Psychoanalytic Society, December 19. Abst. in *Psychoanal. Quart.*, 31:300-302, 1962.

—— (1963), Psychoanalytic Implications of Recent Experimental Research on Sleep and Dreaming. Read at the New York Academy of Medicine, October 31.

—— (1965), Psychoanalytic Implications of Recent Research on Sleep and Dreaming. *J. Amer. Psychoanal. Assn.*, 13:197-303.

—— GROSS, J., & ZUCH, J. (1965), A Cycle of Penile Erection Synchronous with Dreaming (REM) Sleep. *Arch. Gen. Psychiat.*, 12:29-45.

—— & PAUL, I. H. (1959), The Effect of Subliminal Visual Stimulation on Images and Dreams: A Validation Study. *J. Amer. Psychoanal. Assn.*, 7:35-83.

FREUD, A. (1936), *The Ego and the Mechanisms of Defense*. New York: International Universities Press, 1946.

—— (1952), The Mutual Influences in the Development of Ego and Id: Introduction to the Discussion. *The Psychoanalytic Study of the Child*, 7:42-51. New York: International Universities Press.

—— (1965), *Normality and Pathology in Childhood: Assessments of Development*. New York: International Universities Press.

FREUD, S. (1892), Early Studies on the Psychical Mechanism of Hysterical Phenomena. *Collected Papers*, 5:25-32. London: Hogarth Press, 1950.

—— (1895), Project for a Scientific Psychology. In: *The Origins of Psychoanalysis*. New York: Basic Books, 1954, pp. 347-455.

—— (1900), The Interpretation of Dreams. *Standard Edition*, 4 & 5. London: Hogarth Press, 1953.

—— (1901), The Psychopathology of Everyday Life. *Standard Edition*, 6. London: Hogarth Press, 1960.

—— (1905a [1901]), Fragment of an Analysis of a Case of Hysteria. *Standard Edition*, 7:3-122. London: Hogarth Press, 1953.

—— (1905b), Jokes and Their Relation to the Unconscious. *Standard Edition*, 8. London: Hogarth Press, 1960.

—— (1905c), Three Essays on the Theory of Sexuality. *Standard Edition*, 7:125-245. London: Hogarth Press, 1953.

—— (1907 [1906]), Delusions and Dreams in Jensen's *Gradiva*. *Standard Edition*, 9:3-95. London: Hogarth Press, 1959.

—— (1909a [1908]), Some General Remarks on Hysterical Attacks. *Standard Edition*, 9:227-234. London: Hogarth Press, 1959.

—— (1909b), Analysis of a Phobia in a Five-year-old Boy. *Standard Edition*, 10:3-149. London: Hogarth Press, 1955.

—— (1909c), Notes upon a Case of Obsessional Neurosis. *Standard Edition*, 10:153-318. London: Hogarth Press, 1955.

—— (1910 [1909]), Five Lectures on Psycho-Analysis. *Standard Edition*, 11:3-56. London: Hogarth Press, 1957.

—— (1911a), Psycho-Analytic Notes on an Autobiographical Account of a Case of Paranoia (Dementia Paranoides). *Standard Edition*, 12:3-82. London: Hogarth Press, 1958.

—— (1911b), Formulations on the Two Principles of Mental Functioning. *Standard Edition*, 12:213-226. London: Hogarth Press, 1958.

—— (1912), The Dynamics of Transference. *Standard Edition*, 12:97-108. London: Hogarth Press, 1958.

—— (1913a [1912-1913]), Totem and Taboo. *Standard Edition*, 13:1-161. London: Hogarth Press, 1955.

—— (1913b), The Claims of Psycho-Analysis to Scientific Interest. *Standard Edition*, 13:165-190. London: Hogarth Press, 1955.

—— (1914), On the History of the Psycho-Analytic Movement. *Standard Edition*, 14:7-66. London: Hogarth Press, 1957.

—— (1915a), Instincts and Their Vicissitudes. *Standard Edition*, 14:111-140. London: Hogarth Press, 1957.

—— (1915b), Repression. *Standard Edition*, 14:141-158. London: *Hogarth Press*, 1957.

—— (1915c), The Unconscious. *Standard Edition*, 14:159-215. London: Hogarth Press, 1957.

—— (1916-1917 [1915-1917]), Introductory Lectures on Psycho-Analysis. *Standard Edition*, 15 & 16. London: Hogarth Press, 1963.

—— (1917a [1915]), A Metapsychological Supplement to the Theory of Dreams. *Standard Edition*, 14:217-235. London: Hogarth Press, 1957.

—— (1917b [1915]), Mourning and Melancholia. *Standard Edition*, 14:237-260. London: Hogarth Press, 1957.

—— (1918 [1914]), From the History of an Infantile Neurosis. *Standard Edition*, 17:3-123. London: Hogarth Press, 1955.

—— (1919), Introduction to *Psycho-Analysis and the War Neuroses*. *Standard Edition*, 17:205-215. London: Hogarth Press, 1955.

—— (1920), Beyond the Pleasure Principle. *Standard Edition*, 18:7-64. London: Hogarth Press, 1955.

—— (1923), The Ego and the Id. *Standard Edition*, 19:3-66. London: Hogarth Press, 1961.

—— (1924a), The Economic Problem of Masochism. *Standard Edition*, 19:157-170. London: Hogarth Press, 1961.

—— (1924b), The Dissolution of the Oedipus Complex. *Standard Edition*, 19:173-179. London: Hogarth Press, 1961.

—— (1925a [1924]), A Note upon the 'Mystic Writing-Pad.' *Standard Edition*, 19:227-232. London: Hogarth Press, 1961.

—— (1925b [1924]), An Autobiographical Study. *Standard Edition*, 20:3-74. London: Hogarth Press, 1959.

—— (1925c), Some Additional Notes on Dream-Interpretation as a Whole. *Standard Edition*, 19:125-138. London: Hogarth Press, 1961.

—— (1926), Inhibitions, Symptoms and Anxiety. *Standard Edition*, 20:77-175. London: Hogarth Press, 1959.

—— (1927), The Future of an Illusion. *Standard Edition*, 21:3-56. London: Hogarth Press, 1961.

—— (1933 [1932]), New Introductory Lectures on Psycho-Analysis. *Standard Edition*, 22:3-182. London: Hogarth Press, 1964.

—— (1937), Analysis Terminable and Interminable. *Standard Edition*, 23:209-253. London: Hogarth Press, 1964.

—— (1939 [1934-1938]), Moses and Monotheism. *Standard Edition*, 23:3-137. London: Hogarth Press, 1964.

—— (1940 [1938]), An Outline of Psycho-Analysis. *Standard Edition*, 23:141-207. London: Hogarth Press, 1964.

—— (1950 [1887-1902]), *The Origins of Psychoanalysis: Letters, Drafts and Notes to Wilhelm Fliess*. New York: Basic Books, 1954.

—— (1960), *The Letters of Sigmund Freud*, ed. E. L. Freud. New York: Basic Books.

GIFFORD, S. (1964), Report on Panel: Repetition Compulsion. *J. Amer. Psychoanal. Assn.*, 12:632-649.

GILL, M. M. (1963), *Topography and Systems in Psychoanalytic Theory* [*Psychological Issues*, Monogr. 10]. New York: International Universities Press.

GLOVER, E. (1947), *Basic Mental Concepts*. London: Imago Publ. Co.

GRANIT, R. (1955), *Receptors and Sensory Perceptions*. New Haven: Yale University Press.

GREENACRE, P. (1960), Considerations Regarding the Parent-Infant Relationship. *Int. J. Psycho-Anal.*, 41:571-584.

—— (1963), Problems of Acting Out in the Transference Relationship. *J. Amer. Acad. Child Psychiat.*, 2:144-159.

—— (1964), Discussion of: Two Contributions to the Theory of Working Through, by B. H. Brodsky. Read at the New York Psychoanalytic Society, October 13. Abst. in *Psychoanal. Quart.*, 34:319-321.

GREENFIELD, N. S. & LEWIS, W. C., eds. (1965), *Psychoanalysis and Current Biological Thought*. Madison: University of Wisconsin Press.

GREENSON, R. R. (1965), The Problem of Working Through. In: *Drives, Affects, Behavior*, Vol. 2, ed. M. Schur. New York: International Universities Press, pp. 277-314.

GROOS, K. (1901), *The Play of Man*. New York: Appleton.

HARTMANN, H. (1933), An Experimental Contribution to the Psychology of Obsessive-Compulsive Neurosis. In: *Essays on Ego Psychology*. New York: International Universities Press, 1964, pp. 404-418.

—— (1939), *Ego Psychology and the Problem of Adaptation,* tr. D. Rapaport [*Journal of the American Psychoanalytic Association Monograph Series, No. 1*]. New York: International Universities Press, 1958.

—— (1947), On Rational and Irrational Action. In: *Essays on Ego Psychology*. New York: International Universities Press, 1964, pp. 37-68.

—— (1948), Comments on the Psychoanalytic Theory of Instinctual Drives. In: *Essays on Ego Psychology*. New York: International Universities Press, 1964, pp. 69-89.

—— (1950), Comments on the Psychoanalytic Theory of the Ego. In: *Essays on Ego Psychology*. New York: International Universities Press, 1964, pp. 113-141.

—— (1952), The Mutual Influences in the Development of Ego and Id. In: *Essays on Ego Development*. New York: International Universities Press, 1964, pp. 155-181.

—— (1953), Contribution to the Metapsychology of Schizophrenia. In: *Essays on Ego Psychology*. New York: International Universities Press, 1964, pp. 182-206.

—— (1955), Notes on the Theory of Sublimation. In: *Essays on Ego Psychology*. New York: International Universities Press, 1964, pp. 215-240.

—— (1956a), Notes on the Reality Principle. In: *Essays on Ego Psychology*. New York: International Universities Press, 1964, pp. 241-267.

[ 207 ]

—— (1956b), The Development of the Ego Concept in Freud's Work. In: *Essays on Ego Psychology*. New York: International Universities Press, 1964, pp. 268-296.

—— (1958), Comments on the Scientific Aspects of Psychoanalysis. In: *Essays on Ego Psychology*. New York: International Universities Press, 1964, pp. 297-317.

—— (1959), Psychoanalysis as a Scientific Theory. In: *Essays on Ego Psychology*. New York: International Universities Press, 1964, pp. 318-350.

—— (1964), *Essays on Ego Psychology: Selected Problems in Psychoanalytic Theory*. New York: International Universities Press.

—— & KRIS, E. (1945), The Genetic Approach in Psychoanalysis. In: *Papers on Psychoanalytic Psychology* [*Psychological Issues*, Monogr. 14]. New York: International Universities Press, 1964, pp. 7-26.

—— —— & LOEWENSTEIN, R. M. (1946), Comments on the Formation of Psychic Structure. In: *Papers on Psychoanalytic Psychology* [*Psychological Issues*, Monogr. 14]. New York: International Universities Press, 1964, pp. 27-55.

—— —— —— (1949), Notes on the Theory of Aggression. In: *Papers on Psychoanalytic Psychology* [*Psychological Issues*, Monogr. 14]. New York: International Universities Press, 1964, pp. 56-85.

—— —— —— (1951), Some Psychoanalytic Comments on "Culture and Personality." In: *Papers on Psychoanalytic Psychology* [*Psychological Issues*, Monogr. 14]. New York: International Universities Press, 1964, pp. 86-116.

HEBB, D. O. (1949), *The Organization of Behavior: A Neuropsychological Theory*. New York: Wiley.

HEISENBERG, W. (1958), The Representation of Nature in Contemporary Physics. *Daedalus*, 87:95-108.

HENDRICK, I. (1942), Instinct and the Ego during Infancy. *Psychoanal. Quart.*, 11:33-58.

HOFFER, W. (1952), The Mutual Influences in the Development of Ego and Id: Earliest Stages. *The Psychoanalytic Study of the Child*, 7:31-41. New York: International Universities Press.

HOLT, R. R. (1962), Beyond Vitalism and Mechanism. Contribution to Panel: The Concept of Psychic Energy, rep. A. H. Modell. *J. Amer. Psychoanal. Assn.*, 11:605-618, 1963.

—— (1965), The Development of the Primary Process: A Structural View. In: *Motives and Thought: Psychoanalytic Essays in Honor of David Rapaport* [*Psychological Issues*]. New York: International Universities Press (in press).

JACOBSEN, C. F., JACOBSEN, M. M., & YOSHIOKA, J. G. (1953), Development of an Infant Chimpanzee during Her First Year. *Comp. Psychol. Monogr.*, 9(41):1-94.

JACOBSON, E. (1953), The Affects and Their Pleasure-Unpleasure Qualities in Relation to the Psychic Discharge Processes. In: *Drives, Affects, Behavior,* Vol. 1, ed. R. M. Loewenstein. New York: International Universities Press, pp. 38-66.

—— (1964), *The Self and the Object World* [*Journal of the American Psychoanalytic Association Monograph Series,* No. 2]. New York: International Universities Press.

JAHODA, M. (1966), Notes on Work. In: *Psychoanalysis: A Generalizing Psychology,* ed. R. M. Loewenstein, L. Newman, M. Schur, & A. J. Solnit. New York: International Universities Press, 622-633.

KAUFMAN, I. C. (1960), Some Ethological Studies of Social Relationships and Conflict Situations. *J. Amer. Psychoanal. Assn.,* 8:671-685.

KESTENBERG, J. (1953), Notes on Ego Development. *Int. J. Psycho-Anal.,* 34:111-122.

KLEIN, G. S. (1965), On Hearing One's Own Voice: An Aspect of Cognitive Control in Spoken Thought. In: *Drives, Affects, Behavior,* Vol. 2, ed. M. Schur. New York: International Universities Press, pp. 87-117.

KRIS, E. (1934), The Psychology of Caricature. In: *Psychoanalytic Explorations in Art.* New York: International Universities Press, 1952, pp. 173-188.

—— (1936), Comments on Spontaneous Artistic Creations by Psychotics. In: *Psychoanalytic Explorations in Art.* New York: International Universities Press, 1952, pp. 87-127.

—— (1939), Laughter as an Expressive Process. In: *Psychoanalytic Explorations in Art.* New York: International Universities Press, 1952, pp. 217-239.

—— (1950), On Preconscious Mental Processes. In: *Psychoanalytic Explorations in Art.* New York: International Universities Press, 1952, pp. 303-318.

—— (1951), Ego Psychology and Interpretation in Psychoanalytic Therapy. *Psychoanal. Quart.,* 20:15-30.

—— (1952a), Approaches to Art. Introduction to *Psychoanalytic Explorations in Art.* New York: International Universities Press, pp. 13-63.

—— (1952b), *Psychoanalytic Explorations in Art.* New York: International Universities Press.

—— & KAPLAN, A. (1948), Aesthetic Ambiguity. In: *Psychoanalytic Explorations in Art.* New York: International Universities Press, 1952, pp. 243-264.

LEHRMAN, D. (1961), Hormonal Regulation of Parental Behavior in Birds and Infrahuman Mammals. In: *Sex and Internal Secretions,* ed. W. C. Young. Baltimore: Williams & Wilkins.

Lewin, K. (1935), *A Dynamic Theory of Personality*. New York: Mc-Graw-Hill.

Lilly, J. C. (1960), The Psychophysiological Basis for Two Kinds of Instincts. *J. Amer. Psychoanal. Assn.*, 8:659-670.

Lipin, T. (1963), The Repetition Compulsion and 'Maturational' Drive-Representatives. *Int. J. Psycho-Anal.*, 44:389-406.

Littman, R. A. (1958), Motives, History and Causes. In: *Nebraska Symposium on Motivation*, ed. M. R. Jones. Lincoln: University of Nebraska Press, pp. 114-168.

Loewenstein, R. M. (1940), The Vital or Somatic Instincts. *Int. J. Psycho-Anal.*, 21:377-400.

—— (1965), Observational Data and Theory in Psychoanalysis. In: *Drives, Affects, Behavior*, Vol. 2, ed. M. Schur. New York: International Universities Press, pp. 38-59.

Lorenz, K. (1937), The Nature of Instinct. In: *Instinctive Behavior*, ed. & tr. C. H. Schiller. New York: International Universities Press, 1957, pp. 129-175.

—— (1952), The Past Twelve Years in the Comparative Study of Behavior. In: *Instinctive Behavior*, ed. & tr. C. H. Schiller. New York: International Universities Press, 1957, pp. 288-310.

—— (1964), *Zur Naturgeschichte der Aggression: Das sogenannte Böse*. Vienna: Dr. Borotha-Schoeler Verlag.

Lustman, S. L. (1956), Rudiments of the Ego. *The Psychoanalytic Study of the Child*, 11:89-98. New York: International Universities Press.

Mahler, M. S. (1963), Thoughts about Development and Individuation. *The Psychoanalytic Study of the Child*, 18:307-324. New York: International Universities Press.

Marcovitz, E. (1963), Report on Panel: The Concept of the Id. *J. Amer. Psychoanal. Assn.*, 11:151-160.

Marcus, H. (1963), The Material Basis of Psychoanalytic Conceptualization: Its Relation to Cybernetics. *J. Hillside Hosp.*, 12:41-49.

Miller, S. C. (1962), Ego-Autonomy in Sensory Deprivation, Isolation, and Stress. *Int. J. Psycho-Anal.*, 43:1-20.

Nunberg, H. (1932), *Principles of Psychoanalysis*. New York: International Universities Press, 1955.

—— (1937), Theory of the Therapeutic Results of Psychoanalysis. In: *Practice and Theory of Psychoanalysis*. New York: International Universities Press, 1961, pp. 165-173.

Peller, L. (1954), Libidinal Phases, Ego Development, and Play. *The Psychoanalytic Study of the Child*, 9:178-198. New York: International Universities Press.

—— (1955), Libidinal Development as Reflected in Play. *Psychoanalysis*, 3(3):3-11.

PETERS, R. S. (1958), *The Concept of Motivation*. New York: Humanities Press.

PIAGET, J. (1936), *The Origins of Intelligence in Children*. New York: International Universities Press, 1952.

RANGELL, L. (1963), Beyond and Between the No and the Yes: A Tribute to Dr. René A. Spitz. In: *Counterpoint: Libidinal Subject and Object*, ed. II. S. Gaskill. New York: International Universities Press, pp. 29-74.

RAPAPORT, D. (1951a), The Conceptual Model of Psychoanalysis. In: *Psychoanalytic Psychiatry and Psychology*, ed. R. P. Knight & C. R. Friedman. New York: International Universities Press, 1954, pp. 221-247.

—— (1951b), ed. & tr., *Organization and Pathology of Thought*. New York: Columbia University Press.

—— (1953), On the Psycho-Analytic Theory of Affects. *Int. J. Psycho-Anal.*, 34:177-198.

—— (1957), Psychoanalysis as a Developmental Psychology. In: *Perspectives in Psychological Theory*, ed. B. Kaplan & S. Wapner. New York: International Universities Press, 1960, pp. 209-255.

—— (1957-1959), Seminars on Elementary Metapsychology, 3 Vols., ed. S. C. Miller. Western New England Institute for Psychoanalysis [mimeographed].

—— (1960a), On the Psychoanalytic Theory of Motivation. In: *Nebraska Symposium on Motivation*, ed. M. R. Jones. Lincoln: University of Nebraska Press, pp. 173-247.

—— (1960b), *The Structure of Psychoanalytic Theory* [*Psychological Issues*, Monogr. 6]. New York: International Universities Press.

—— & GILL, M. M. (1959), The Points of View and Assumptions of Metapsychology. *Int. J. Psycho-Anal.*, 40:153-162.

RITVO, L. B. (1965), Darwin as the Source of Freud's Neo-Lamarckianism. *J. Amer. Psychoanal. Assn.*, 13:499-517.

SCHILDER, P. (1930), Studies Concerning the Psychology and Symptomatology of General Paresis. In: *Organization and Pathology of Thought*, ed. & tr. D. Rapaport. New York: Columbia University Press, 1951, pp. 519-580.

SCHNEIRLA, T. C. (1956), Interrelationships of the "Innate" and the "Acquired" in Instinctive Behavior. In: *L'Instinct dans le Comportement des Animaux et de l'Homme*. Paris: Massin, pp. 387-452.

—— (1957), The Concept of Development in Comparative Psychology. In: *The Concept of Development: An Issue in the Study of Human Behavior*, ed. C. B. Harms. Minneapolis: University of Minnesota Press, pp. 78-108.

[ 211 ]

—— (1959), An Evolutionary and Developmental Theory of Biphasic Processes Underlying Approach and Withdrawal. In: *Nebraska Symposium on Motivation,* ed. M. R. Jones. Lincoln: University of Nebraska Press, pp. 1-41.

SCHUR, M. (1953), The Ego in Anxiety. In: *Drives, Affects, Behavior,* Vol. 1, ed. R. M. Loewenstein. New York: International Universities Press, pp. 67-103.

—— (1955), Comments on the Metapsychology of Somatization. *The Psychoanalytic Study of the Child,* 10:119-164. New York: International Universities Press.

—— (1958), The Ego and the Id in Anxiety. *The Psychoanalytic Study of the Child,* 13:190-220. New York: International Universities Press.

—— (1960a), Phylogenesis and Ontogenesis of Affect- and Structure-Formation and the Phenomenon of Repetition Compulsion. *Int. J. Psycho-Anal.,* 41:275-287.

—— (1960b), Chairman's Introduction to Panel: Psychoanalysis and Ethology, rep. M. Ostow. *J. Amer. Psychoanal. Assn.,* 8:526-534.

—— (1961a), Animal Research Panel, 1960: A Psychoanalyst's Comments. *Amer. J. Orthopsychiat.,* 31:276-291.

—— (1961b), Discussion in Panel: Aggression and Symptom Formation, rep. S. D. Lipton. *J. Amer. Psychoanal. Assn.,* 9:585-592.

—— (1962), The Theory of the Parent-Infant Relationship. *Int. J. Psycho-Anal.,* 43:243-245.

—— (1963), Discussion in Panel: The Concept of the Id, rep. E. Marcowitz. *J. Amer. Psychoanal. Assn.,* 11:151-160.

—— (1964), Discussion of: A Cycle of Penile Erection Synchronous with Dreaming Sleep, by C. Fisher. Read at the New York Psychoanalytic Society, March 17. Abst. in *Psychoanal. Quart.,* 33:614-617.

—— (1965a), Editor's Introduction: Marie Bonaparte, 1882-1960. In: *Drives, Affects, Behavior,* Vol. 2, ed. M. Schur. New York: International Universities Press, pp. 9-20.

—— (1965b), Discussion of: Some Aspects of Scientific Theory Construction and Psychoanalysis, by S. A. Guttman. Read at the New York Psychoanalytic Society, February 9. Abst. in *Psychoanal. Quart.,* 34:631-633.

—— (1966), *The Problem of Death in Freud's Writings and Life.* New York: International Universities Press (in press).

—— & RITVO, L. B. (1966), The Concept of Development and Evolution in Psychoanalysis. In: *Development and Evolution of Behavior: In Honor of T. C. Schneirla,* Vol. I, Essays Presented to

T. C. Schneirla, ed. L. Aronson, D. Lehrman, J. S. Rosenblatt, & E. Tobach. San Francisco: W. H. Freeman (in press).

SIMMEL, E. (1918), *Kriegsneurosen und psychisches Trauma.* Munich & Leipzig: Otto Nemnich.

SPITZ, R. A. (1937), Wiederholung, Rhythmus, Langeweile. *Imago,* 23:171-196.

—— (1959), *A Genetic Field Theory of Ego Formation.* New York: International Universities Press.

—— (1965), *The First Year of Life: A Psychoanalytic Study of Normal and Deviant Development of Object Relations.* New York: International Universities Press.

STEIN, M. H. (1965), States of Consciousness in the Analytic Situation: Including a Note on the Traumatic Dream. In: *Drives, Affects, Behavior,* Vol. 2, ed. M. Schur. New York: International Universities Press, pp. 60-86.

STONE, L. (1961), *The Psychoanalytic Situation.* New York: International Universities Press.

STRACHEY, J. (1961), Editor's Introduction to *The Ego and the Id. Standard Edition,* 19:3-11. London: Hogarth Press.

THORPE, W. (1956), *Learning and Instincts in Animals.* Cambridge: Harvard University Press.

TINBERGEN, N. (1951), *The Study of Instinct.* Oxford: University Press.

VON UEXKÜLL, J. (1934), A Stroll Through the World of Animals and Men. In: *Instinctive Behavior,* ed. & tr. C. H. Schiller. New York: International Universities Press, 1957, pp. 5-80.

WAELDER, R. (1932), The Psychoanalytical Theory of Play. *Psychoanal. Quart.,* 2:208-224, 1933.

—— (1960), *Basic Theory of Psychoanalysis.* New York: International Universities Press, pp. 97-103.

WERNER, H. (1948), *Comparative Psychology of Mental Development.* New York: International Universities Press, 1957.

WHITE, R. W. (1959), Motivation Reconsidered: The Concept of Competence. *Psychol. Rev.,* 66:297-333.

—— (1963), *Ego and Reality in Psychoanalytic Theory* [*Psychological Issues,* Monogr. 11]. New York: International Universities Press.

WOLFF, P. H. (1959), Observations on Newborn Infants. *Psychosom. Med.,* 21:110-118.

—— (1960), *The Developmental Psychologies of Jean Piaget and Psychoanalysis* [*Psychological Issues,* Monogr. 5]. New York: International Universities Press.

# Index

This index is arranged by authors' names in alphabetical sequence. The bulk of the subjects treated in this monograph will be found under the names of S. Freud, Hartmann, and Schur.

[ 215 ]

*Monographs of the*
*Journal of the American Psychoanalytic Association*
*1958–1966*

## No. 1

EGO PSYCHOLOGY AND THE PROBLEM
OF ADAPTATION

By **Heinz Hartmann**

Translated by **David Rapaport**

## No. 2

THE SELF AND THE OBJECT WORLD

By **Edith Jacobson**

## No. 3

PSYCHOANALYTIC CONCEPTS AND THE
STRUCTURAL THEORY

By **Jacob A. Arlow** and **Charles Brenner**

## No. 4

THE ID AND THE REGULATORY PRINCIPLES
OF MENTAL FUNCTIONING

By **Max Schur**

# CHAPTER
# NINETEEN

THE NEXT STEP was to get the house ready for his arrival. He wouldn't come before dark. He was afraid to move around the city in daylight even though she'd told him no one was looking for him, no one wanted to find him. He was safe: the case was over and Valenzuela was dead. It was sheer luck that she'd chosen to buy this particular house. The California mission style suited her purpose—adobe walls as much as two feet thick, heavy tiled roof, enclosed court, and more important than anything else, iron grillwork across the windows to keep people out. Or in.

She returned to the front bedroom and her interrupted task of fixing it up. The cartons, marked Salvation Army in Devon's small square printing, were nearly all unpacked. The old map had been taped to the door: BEYOND THIS POINT ARE MONSTERS. Robert's clothes hung in the closet, his surfing posters and college pennants decorated the walls, his glasses were on the top of the bureau, the lenses carefully polished, and his boots were beside the bed as if he'd just stepped out of them. Robert had never seen this room, but it belonged to him.

When she finished unpacking the cartons she dragged them to the rear of the house and piled them on the service porch. Then she brewed some coffee and took it into the living room to wait until the sun set. She'd forgotten about lunch and when dinner time came she felt light-headed and a little dizzy, but she still wasn't hungry. She made another pot of coffee and sat for a long time listening to the little brass horses dancing in the wind and the bamboo clawing at the iron grills across the windows. At dusk she switched on all the lights in the house so that if he was outside watching he could see she was alone.

It was nearly nine o'clock when she heard the tapping at the front door. She went to open it and he was standing there as he'd been standing a hundred times in her mind throughout the day. He was thinner than she remembered, almost emaciated, as if some greedy parasite had taken up residence in his body and was intercepting his food. She said, "I thought you might have changed your mind."

"I need the money."

"Come in."

"We can talk out here."

"It's too cold. Come in," she said again, and this time he obeyed.

He looked too tired to argue. There were dark blue semicircles under his eyes, almost the color of the work clothes he wore, and he kept sniffling and wiping his nose with his sleeve like a child with a cold. She suspected that he'd picked up a drug habit along the way, perhaps in some Mexican prison, perhaps in one of the local *barrios*. She wouldn't ask him where he'd spent the long year and what he'd done to survive. Her only questions would be important ones.

''Where is he, Felipe?''

He turned and stared at the door closing behind him as if he had a sudden impulse to pull it open and run back into the darkness.

''Don't be nervous,'' she said. ''I promised you on the phone that I wouldn't press charges, wouldn't even tell anyone I'd seen you. All I want is the truth, the truth in exchange for the money. That's a fair bargain, isn't it?''

''I guess.''

''Where is he?''

''The sea, I put him in the sea.''

''Robert was a very strong swimmer. He might have—''

''No. He was dead, wrapped in blankets.''

Her hands reached up and touched her face as though she could feel pieces of it loosening. ''You killed him, Felipe.''

''It wasn't my fault. He attacked me, he was going to murder me like he did the—''

''Then you wrapped him in blankets.''

''Yes.''

''Robert was a big man, you couldn't have done that by yourself.'' Her voice was cool and calm. ''You must come and sit down quietly and tell me about it.''

''We can talk here.''

''I'm paying a great deal of money for this conversation.''

I might as well be comfortable during the course of it. Come along."

After a moment's hesitation he followed her into the living room. She'd forgotten how short he was, hardly bigger than Robert had been at fifteen, the year he suddenly started to grow. Felipe was twenty now, it was too late for him to start growing. He would always look like a boy, a sad strange sick little boy with a ravenous appetite and poor digestion.

"Sit down, Felipe."

"No."

"Very well."

He stood in front of the fireplace, pale and tense. On the backgammon table between the two wing chairs the game was still in progress but no one had made a move for a long time. Dust covered the board, the thrown dice, the plastic players.

She saw him staring at the board. "Do you play backgammon?"

"No."

"I taught Robert the game when he was fifteen."

Backgammon wasn't the only game Robert had learned at fifteen. The others weren't so innocent, the players were real and each throw of the dice was irrevocable. During the past year she had spent whole days thinking of how differently she would handle things if she had another chance; she would protect him, keep him away from corrupters like Ruth, even if she had to lock him in his room.

She said, "Where have you been living?"

"Tijuana."

"And you saw my reward offer in the paper?"

"Yes."

"Weren't you afraid of walking into a trap by coming here tonight?"

"Some. But I figured you didn't want the police around any more than I did."

"Are you on drugs, Felipe?"

He didn't answer.

"Amphetamines?"

His eyes had begun to water and he seemed to be looking at her through little crystal balls. There was no future in any of them. "It's none of your business. All I want is to earn the money and get out of here."

"Please don't shout. I hate angry sounds. I've had to cover up so many of them. Yes, yes, I still play the piano," she said, as if he'd asked, as if he cared. "I make quite a few mistakes, but it doesn't matter because nobody hears me, and the walls are too thick. . . . Why did you kill him, Felipe?"

"It wasn't my fault, none of it was my fault. I wasn't even living at the ranch when it happened. I only went back that night to try and get some money from my father. I was a little roughed up from fighting—I ran into Luis Lopez in a bar in Boca—and that put my father in a bad mood. He wouldn't give me a nickel, so I decided to go over to the mess hall and touch Lum Wing for a loan. If my father had given me some money, like he should have, I'd never have been anywhere near that mess hall, I'd never—"

"I don't want to hear your excuses. Just report what happened."

"Rob—Mr. Osborne saw the light in the mess hall and came in to investigate. He asked me what I was doing there and I told him. He said Lum Wing was asleep and I wasn't to bother him. And I said why not, money's no use to an old man like that, all he does is carry it around. Anyway, we started arguing back and forth."

"Did you ask Robert for money?"

"No more than what he owed me."

"Robert had borrowed money from you?"

"No, but he owed it to me for my loyalty. I never said a word to anybody about seeing him come in from the field right after his father's accident. He was carrying a two-by-four and it had blood on it. I had climbed up one of the date palms looking for a rat's nest and I watched him throw the two-by-four into the reservoir. I was just a kid, ten years old, but I was smart enough to keep my mouth shut." He blinked, remembering. "I was always climbing up crazy places where no one would think of looking. That's how I found out about him and Mrs. Bishop, I used to see them meet. It went on for years, until he got sick of her and she walked into the river. It was no accident, like the police claimed ... Well, I never said a word about those things to anybody. I figured he owed me something for my loyalty."

"In other words, you tried to blackmail him."

"I asked him to pay me a debt."

"And he refused."

"He came at me, he hurt me bad. He'd have killed me if it hadn't been for the knife I took from Luis Lopez. I hardly remember the fight, except he suddenly fell on the floor and there was blood all over. I could tell he was dead. I didn't know what to do except get away from there fast. I started to run but I caught my sleeve on a yucca spike outside the door. I was trying to get loose when I looked around and saw my father. He was staring at the knife in my hand. He said, 'What have you done?' and I said I got mixed up in a fight between Mr. Osborne and one of the migrants."

"Did he believe you?"

"Yes. But he said no one else would. I had a bad reputation for fighting and Mr. Osborne was an Anglo and things would go hard for me."

"So he helped you."

"Yes. He thought we should make it look like a robbery, so he gave me Mr. Osborne's wallet and told me to throw it away like I was to throw away the knife. He brought some blankets from the bunkhouse and we wrapped Mr.

Osborne in them and put him in the back of the old red pickup. My father said no one would miss it. That was when the dog suddenly appeared. I kicked at him to make him go away and he bit me, he bit me on the leg, and when I drove off he chased the truck. I don't remember the truck hitting him."

"Did you leave the ranch before the migrants returned from Boca de Rio?"

"Yes."

"And of course it was quite simple for Estivar to handle them. He had hired them, he paid them, he gave them their orders; he spoke their language and was a member of their race. All he had to do was tell them the boss had been murdered and they'd better get out of there fast if they wanted to avoid trouble. Their papers were forged, they couldn't afford to argue, so they left."

"Yes."

"And you, Felipe, what did you do?"

"I dropped the body off the end of a pier, then I drove across the border. It was the beginning of a weekend, there were hundreds of other people waiting to cross. No one was looking for me and no one at the ranch noticed the pickup was missing. If they had, my father would have covered for me."

"I'm sure he would. Yes, Estivar is very sentimental about his sons. You can hear it in his voice when he says *my sons, my sons,* as if he were the only one who had ever had a son—" Her voice had begun to tremble and she paused for a minute to regain control. "And that's the whole story, Felipe?"

"Yes."

"It hardly seems worth all the money I offered, especially since there were two quite serious mistakes in it."

"I told you the truth. I want my money."

"Both mistakes concerned Robert. He didn't get sick of Ruth Bishop. On the contrary, they were planning to go away together. I naturally couldn't allow that. Why, she was old enough to be his mother. I ran her off the place like a stray bitch . . . The other mistake was about the two-by-four you saw Robert throw into the reservoir. It had blood on it, his father's blood, but Robert hadn't put it there. He was protecting me. We must keep the record straight."

"I want my money," he said again. "I earned it."

"And you'll get it."

"When?"

"Right now. The safe is in the front bedroom. You can open it yourself."

He shook his head. "I don't know how. I never—"

"You just turn the dial according to my instructions. Come along."

The safe was built into the floor of the bedroom closet and concealed by a rectangle of carpeting. She removed the carpeting, then stood aside while Felipe knelt in front of the safe.

"Left to three," she said. "Right to five. Left to—"

"I can't make out the numbers."

"Are you short-sighted?"

"No. It's too dark in here. I need a flashlight."

"I think you're short-sighted." She picked up Robert's horn-rimmed glasses from the bureau. "Here, you'll be able to see better with these."

"No, I don't need—"

"Try them on. You may be surprised at the difference."

"I have good eyes, I've always had good eyes."

But even while he was protesting she was putting the glasses in position on his face. They slid down past the bridge of his nose and she pushed them back in place. "There. Isn't that an improvement? Now we'll start over. Left to three. Right to five. Left to eight. Right to two."

The safe didn't open.

"Gracious, I hope I haven't forgotten the combination. Perhaps it's left to five to begin with. Try again. Don't

*Beyond This Point Are Monsters*

hurry it. I can't let you rush off immediately anyway." She reached out and touched the top of his head very gently.

"We haven't seen each other for a long time, son."

DURING THE NIGHT one of the neighbors woke to the sound of a piano and went to sleep again.

# ABOUT THE AUTHOR

**Margaret Millar** is internationally known as a novelist of mystery and suspense. Her books have been widely translated in Europe, Asia and South America. Beast in View was given the Edgar Allan Poe award by her fellow Mystery Writers of America in 1956, and the following year she served as president of that organization. In 1965 she received a Los Angeles Times Woman of the Year award for "outstanding achievement."

Born in Canada, Mrs. Millar was educated in classics at the University of Toronto. In 1938 she married Kenneth Millar, whose books are published under the name of Ross Macdonald.

In the fall of 1958 the Millars moved into a house in a wooded canyon just outside Santa Barbara. Here she writes for three or four hours a day and, for relaxation, enjoys swimming, sailing, gardening and bird-watching. Both the Millars are active conservationists and founding members of the Santa Barbara Audubon Society; Mrs. Millar has written a book entitled The Birds and the Beasts Were There.

# 1

## *The Concept Id*

I HAVE already alluded to the extent to which ego psychology has dominated our discussions of structural concepts. And yet as late as 1936 Anna Freud introduced *The Ego and the Mechanisms of Defense* with the following statement:

> There have been periods in the development of psychoanalytical science when the theoretical study of the individual ego was distinctly unpopular. . . . Whenever interest was transferred from the deeper to the more superficial psychic strata—. . . from the id to the ego—it was felt that here was a beginning of apostasy from psycho-analysis as a whole [p. 3].

In 1952 Hartmann pointed out: "Only in the 20s was ego psychology explicitly defined as a legitimate chapter of analysis" (p. 156).

The "ascendancy" of the ego in Freud's thinking was a very gradual process. However, an awareness of the ego's importance was always there, and even semantically formulated. The following (unpublished) letter to Jung (written on December 19, 1909)[1] indicates that what might have appeared to be lack of insight was actually conscious restraint:

> . . . We have already agreed that the basic mechanism of neurosogenesis is the antagonism between the instinctual

[1] I am indebted to the Sigmund Freud Copyright Ltd. for permission to publish this letter.

[ 17 ]

drives—the ego as the repressing [force], the libido as the repressed. The old article on anxiety neurosis was the first to present this point of view. It is remarkable, though, that we human beings find it so difficult to focus attention equally on both of these opposing drives [instinctual camps], so that we carry this antagonism between ego and libido right into our observations, which should impartially encompass both of them. Thus far I have really described only the repressed, which is the novel, the unknown, as Cato did when he sided with the *causa victa*. I hope I have not forgotten that there also exists a *victrix*. Here Adler's psychology invariably sees only the repressing agency and therefore describes the "sensitivity," this attitude of the ego toward the libido, as the basic cause of neurosis. Now I find you on the same path, using nearly identical words. That is, because I have not sufficiently studied the ego, you are running the risk of not doing justice to the libido which I have evaluated.

[. . . Dass der Grundmechanismus des Neurotischwerdens der Gegensatz der Triebe ist, das Ich als das Verdrängende, die Libido als das Verdrängte, darüber haben wir uns ja schon geeinigt. Der alte Aufsatz über die Angstneurose spricht diesen Standpunkt zuerst aus. Nun ist es aber merkwürdig, dass wir Menschen es so schwer dazu bringen, die Aufmerksamkeit gleichmässig auf beide Trieblager gerichtet zu halten und den Gegensatz zwischen Ich und Libido auch in die Beobachtung fortsetzen, die beide unparteiisch umfassen soll. Ich habe bisher eigentlich immer nur das Verdrängte beschrieben als das Neue, Ungekannte, als der Cato, der sich für die causa victa einsetzt. Ich hoffe, ich habe nicht vergessen, dass es eine victrix gibt. Adlers Psychologie hier sieht immer nur das Verdrängende und beschreibt daher die "Empfindlichkeit", diese Attitude des Ich gegen die Libido als Grundbedingung der Neurose. Auf demselben Weg finde ich nun auch Sie, fast mit dem gleichen Wort. Dh. Ueber dem von mir nicht genügend studierten Ich geraten Sie auch in Gefahr, der von mir gewürdigten Libido Unrecht zu thun.]